Mom, I Don't Know Medicare Either

The Adult Child's Guide to Medicare for Immigrant Parents

Lawrence Lee

New American Family Advisors

Mom, I Don't Know Medicare Either The Adult Child's Guide to Medicare for Immigrant Parents - Green Cards, Enrollment, Penalties, and the Coverage They've Earned by Lawrence Lee

First edition, 2026

ISBN: 979-8-9974624-5-1

Published by New American Family Advisors

For permissions, bulk orders, or inquiries, contact: info@newamericanfamilyadvisors.net

Disclaimer

This book is intended for general educational and informational purposes only. It is not legal, immigration, tax, financial, investment, insurance, or medical advice, and it is not a substitute for advice from a qualified professional who is familiar with your specific situation.

The author is not acting as your attorney, accredited immigration representative, financial advisor, insurance agent, or health care provider, and reading this book does not create any professional or advisory relationship.

Medicare, Medicaid, Social Security, immigration, and tax rules, along with premiums, penalties, income and asset limits, fees, benefit amounts, and eligibility requirements, change frequently and vary by state and by individual circumstances. Every figure, rule, and program described in this book is believed to be accurate as of the time of writing in 2026, but such information can and does change, sometimes substantially, after publication. Some rules described here were subject to pending changes or legal challenges as this book was written.

Before making any decision or taking any action based on this book, you should verify the current rules with the official sources, including medicare.gov, ssa.gov, and uscis.gov, and consult a qualified professional such as a licensed Medicare or insurance agent, an elder-law or immigration attorney, an accredited immigration representative, a benefits counselor, or your State Health Insurance Assistance Program (SHIP).

This book is not affiliated with, endorsed by, or sponsored by the Centers for Medicare & Medicaid Services, the Social Security Administration, U.S. Citizenship and Immigration Services, or any other government agency. All program names and trademarks are the property of their respective owners.

The stories and characters in this book are illustrative. Any examples, names, dialogues, and scenarios are composites created to explain concepts and do not depict any specific real person. Any resemblance to actual individuals is coincidental. Certain dollar figures in worked examples are clearly labeled as invented for illustration and are not real Medicare amounts.

The author and publisher make no representations or warranties with respect to the accuracy, completeness, or applicability of the contents, and disclaim any liability, loss, or risk, personal or otherwise, incurred as a consequence, directly or indirectly, of the use or application of any of the contents of this book.

For my very best girls - Jeongyoon, Erin, and Hannah.

And for the children who became their parents' guides.

Contents

Introduction

When I began teaching Medicare to insurance agents, I did not expect to become the person they called when they got stuck. But that is what ended up happening. Agents repeatedly referred their hardest cases to me for a solution, and as those cases piled up, I started to see a pattern that changed how I understand this entire field.

What I realized is that there are, in truth, two different Medicare territories.

The first is Medicare for regular American seniors – people born and raised in the United States – who have worked here their whole lives. It is a large and dominant market, and nearly every Medicare agent wants to work in it. It is the Medicare that every guide, seminar, and brochure is written for.

The second is something more foreign. It is Medicare for immigrant seniors, and it barely resembles the first. The rules bend in ways that surprise even experienced agents: residence clocks, sponsor deeming, premiums for coverage that other seniors get free, five-year waits, public-charge fears. Very few agents have the experience to solve the problems these families face. When I went looking for a guide, a resource, anything written for this second territory, I found almost nothing.

That absence is a kind of perfect storm. On one side are families who are unfamiliar with Medicare or the U.S. social-benefits system, because it was never part of the world they came from. On the other side are a limited number of advisors properly equipped to help them. And caught in the middle are the adult children, who, despite being well-educated and fluent in English, still cannot find their way through because no one ever exposed them to this system either. They are trying to help their parents through a maze they were never taught to read.

The stakes in that maze are high. Handled wrong, or missed entirely, the rules in this second territory can cost a family tens of thousands of dollars over a retirement, and some of those losses can never be undone. Handled well, almost all of them are preventable. That gap, between what a family loses by not knowing and what it keeps by planning, is the reason this book exists.

So I have gathered what I have learned from years of teaching Medicare and working through the cases no one else could solve, and put it into one place. This comprehensive guide is written for the millions of immigrant families who have to navigate a system that was never designed with them in mind.

A few words on how to read this book. Each chapter opens with a short scene from a family like yours and closes with an action checklist you can follow immediately. You do not have to read front to back; the checklists alone will move you forward. But the chapters are sequenced for a reason, and the order is the plan. It is built around the years your parent has spent as a green-card holder, treating them not as dead time but as a window to be used in reference to different policies and regulations.

One caution runs through every chapter: verify the current rule before you act. I have worked to make every figure and rule here accurate as of 2026, but a book is a mere snapshot, while your family's decisions happen in real time. When your moment comes, confirm the current rule at the official source and lean on the professionals this book will help you find.

Finally, remember that this is not only paperwork. It is one of the ways a child cares for a parent who once cared for them. The work is real, and it can feel heavy, but you are not the first to carry it, and you no longer have to carry it blind. That is what this book is for. Turn the page, and let's begin.

Part One · Before You Begin

Chapter 1

"Sofia, Can You Read for Me?" - Recognizing the Moment

"Sofia, my phone says your mom's birthday is coming up next month. Any idea what we should get her?"

Sofia barely looked up from her laptop. Leo's question tugged at something. A text from Mom last week, about something. Not the birthday. Something else. She made a mental note to find it later, knowing she probably wouldn't.

"Thanks, Leo. Let's just take her to that restaurant she loved last year." She was already moving on. "Did you check Luna's weekend schedule? She's got a big game Saturday. You'll need to take her."

"Saturday? I've got that golf outing with James. Sofia, I swear I told you about this two weeks ago. Don't say you didn't hear it."

"Leo, are you serious?" She didn't even turn around. "I told you three weeks ago I have a company event Saturday."

It was just another lively, ordinary, impossible morning. Three calendars collided before the coffee was gone cold. Somewhere in the noise, a text from her mother went unanswered as usual.

She finally found out what that text was about a month later, on the night of her mother's birthday dinner.

She had dropped her mother back home and lingered a moment to say good night while the older woman hurried off to the restroom. That was when the pile caught her eye. A small heap of envelopes sat in the corner of the kitchen table, half-hidden under a basket of mail. The strange part was that she had been seeing it for weeks without ever really seeing it.

Sofia picked one up. Social Security Administration. The envelope had been opened, then carefully reclosed, the way her mother handled things she didn't understand but couldn't bring herself to throw away. Inside was a notice with a deadline. The deadline had passed eleven days ago.

When her mother returned, Sofia held up the letter. "Mamá, what is this?"

Her mother's face did something Sofia had never seen. A flicker of shame, quickly hidden. "I don't know, mija," she said quietly. "I was waiting for you. There are many. I can't read them." She paused. "Sofia, can you read for me?"

In that moment, Sofia understood three things at once. First, that her mother had been quietly drowning in paperwork she couldn't decipher, too proud or too frightened to ask. Second, that some of these letters mattered, in ways that could cost money or coverage. And third, that no one was coming to handle this. Not a social worker, not a relative, not the government. It was going to be her. The reading, the deciphering, the deciding. All of it. Her.

The same daughter who couldn't find a free Saturday was now holding a deadline that had already passed.

If you are holding this book, you have probably had your own version of that evening.

The Day the Roles Reverse

There is a moment every immigrant family reaches, though almost no one names it when it arrives. It is the day the child becomes the parent's guide to the country.

For most of your life, the direction of help ran one way. Your parents brought you here, or they came so that you could be born here. They navigated a language that wasn't theirs, signed papers they only half understood, took jobs beneath their training, and absorbed a thousand small humiliations so that you would never have to. They were the ones who figured things out.

And then, slowly and then all at once, the current reverses. The forms get more complicated. The systems get more important. Health coverage, retirement income, long-term care. That importance grows at exactly the moment your parents' ability to fight through them on their own begins to fade. The English that was good enough for the grocery store and the parent-teacher conference is not good enough for a Medicare enrollment notice or a Social Security earnings dispute. And so they wait. They wait for you.

This role reversal is hard for any family. For immigrant families it carries an extra weight, because it is a system your parents were never taught, in a language that was never theirs, with rules that treat them differently than they treat citizens. You are not just helping your mother read a letter. You are acting as the financial advisor, the social worker, the case manager, and the translator. Other families might have all of these. Your family has folded them into one person. You.

That is a heavy thing to carry. This book exists to make it lighter, and to make sure that carrying it does not cost your family tens of thousands of dollars it did not have to lose.

Why the Quiet Pile Is So Expensive

Every family has a version of the quiet pile. The unopened mail, the deferred decision, the "we'll deal with it later." In most families, the cost of procrastination is mild. A late fee. A rescheduled appointment. An annoying phone call.

For immigrant seniors, the quiet pile is uniquely expensive, and for a reason most people never see coming. Many of the most important deadlines in this system are one-time doors that close permanently, and several of them carry penalties that last for the rest of your parent's life.

Consider just a few of the things hiding in a pile like your mother's.

A missed Medicare enrollment window can trigger a late-enrollment penalty that is added to the monthly premium for life. This is not a one-time fine. A few unopened envelopes can quietly convert into thousands of dollars over a retirement.

A five-year clock can go unstarted. As you will see in Chapter 6, immigrant seniors live under two different five-year rules, and for some benefits the clock only starts when certain paperwork is filed. A pile on a kitchen table can mean a clock that should have started two years ago still has not.

A benefit your parent qualified for can go unclaimed. A Medicare Savings Program, Part D Extra Help (LIS, Low-Income Subsidy), in some cases SSI (Supplemental Security Income), worth thousands of dollars a year, can sit unclaimed because the application was in the pile.

A public-charge or sponsorship question can be answered wrong, or a benefit can be applied for at the wrong moment, in a way that complicates a future green-card renewal or citizenship application.

This is the hard truth that organizes this entire book. In the immigrant senior world, time is money, and missed time is often money you can never get back. The pile is disorganized and expensive.

Luckily, there is good news, and there is a lot of good news in these pages. Almost every one of these losses is preventable with a plan and a little warning. That is what you are holding.

What This Book Is (and What It Isn't)

Let us be clear that this book is not a generic Medicare manual. There are hundreds of those, and your parents do not fit the assumptions behind any of them. The standard guide assumes the reader is a U.S. citizen, has worked in this country for forty quarters, reads English comfortably, and has no sponsor, no five-year clock, and no public-charge worry in the background. Hand that book to an immigrant family and most of it is either irrelevant or quietly misleading. Chapter 2 walks through exactly which hidden assumptions trip immigrant families up.

This book is built on a different assumption. Your parent became a lawful permanent resident later in life. The path to full benefits runs through time and citizenship. And you, the adult child, are the one actually doing the work.

So this is a five-year action plan for the adult child. Its central insight is that the years your parent spends as a green-card holder before citizenship, what we will call the "bridge years," are not dead time to be endured. They are a window to be used. Use them to build work credits, to start the right clocks, to avoid the expensive mistakes, to bridge coverage affordably, and to march steadily toward the one thing that unlocks everything. The book is organized around making those years count.

The Plan Behind This Book

Every chapter is built the same way on the page. It opens with a short scene from a family like yours, and it closes with an action checklist of concrete steps you can take this week. You do not have to read front to back. If you are in a hurry, the checklists alone will move you forward. But the chapters are sequenced for a reason, and the order is the plan.

That plan rests on four ideas. If you understand these four, you understand the spine of the whole book.

The first idea is the bridge-years spine. Most of this book is organized around a simple question. How does your family survive the years before citizenship with the least cost and the most protection? Citizenship is the destination, but it takes at least five years of permanent residence to get there, and your parent needs coverage, income, and protection during those years. Parts 3 through 6 are a survival map for the bridge: eligibility, affordability, penalty avoidance, and the safety net, in that order.

The second idea is the three layers of dignity. When it comes to actual coverage, we will think in three layers. The Foundation is the core Medicare coverage that keeps your parent's care from depending on luck. Protection is the supplemental layer that shields the family from catastrophic out-of-pocket costs. Legacy is the long-term-care question, the gap Medicare does not cover, that determines whether a long illness drains everything your parents built. Part 5 takes these one at a time.

The third idea is the citizenship throughline. Where naturalization genuinely changes an outcome, we will say so plainly, in a short box called "How citizenship changes this." You will not see that box in every chapter, and that is deliberate. It appears only where citizenship actually alters your parent's eligibility, cost, or risk, so that when you do see it, it means something. Citizenship removes the five-year bar, ends sponsor deeming, and erases public-charge worry. We treat naturalization as the master key it is, and Chapter 22 turns it into a step-by-step plan.

The fourth idea is the recurring agent resource. In the chapters where a knowledgeable professional actually does the work, you will see a callout marked "Where a Medicare agent helps," naming the specific job. Like the citizenship box, it appears only where it is real, not as decoration. The next section explains why that help can be free.

Where a Medicare Agent Helps

Here is something most adult children do not realize until late. You are not required to become a Medicare expert. There are professionals whose entire job is to help your parent choose and enroll in coverage, and for the most common kinds of help, they cost your family nothing.

A licensed Medicare insurance agent helps people compare plans, understand enrollment windows, and avoid penalties. A good one who understands immigrant situations can be the single most valuable ally you find. Here is the part that surprises people. For most plan enrollments, you do not pay the agent at all. Agents are paid a commission by the insurance company when they enroll someone in a plan, and the premium your parent pays is the same whether you use an agent or not. Medicare sets the rules so that going through an agent does not raise your cost. The agent is a free, ongoing guide that the system has already paid for.

Not all agents are equal, and there are honest limits to what an agent does. An agent is paid to help with insurance plans, not to give immigration advice, file your parent's taxes, or determine SSI eligibility. The best agents are independent, so they can compare many companies rather than sell one. They speak your parent's language or work with someone who does. And they have real experience with non-citizen clients. Chapter 19 is devoted to finding the right one and building a small team around them: an agent, and where needed an immigration attorney, a SHIP (State Health Insurance Assistance Program) counselor, and a tax professional.

For now, hold on to this. The moment you start to feel that the pile on the kitchen table is too much for one person, that feeling is correct. This book shows you how to work harder as a team

Action Checklist

- ☐ Gather the pile. Collect every piece of government mail your parent has received from Social Security, Medicare, Medicaid, and USCIS (U.S. Citizenship and Immigration Services), even the unopened ones. Put it all in one place.
- ☐ Sort by sender, not by date. Make a stack for Social Security/SSA (Social Security Administration), one for Medicare/CMS (Centers for Medicare & Medicaid Services), one for Medicaid/state, and one for immigration/USCIS. You are looking for the shape of the situation, not reading every word yet.
- ☐ Flag anything with a deadline, and note whether it has already passed. Do not panic over a passed deadline. Some can be reopened. Just identify them.

- ☐ Do not apply for or cancel anything yet. Before you file any benefit application, read Chapter 4 on the three landmines. A wrong move here can be costly.
- ☐ Appoint a project manager. In most families, this ends up being one person. If that is you, say so out loud to your family, so the responsibility and the authority to make calls are clear.
- ☐ Schedule one hour this week to read Chapters 2 through 4. They explain why standard advice fails your family, what the real stakes are, and the three mistakes to avoid before you do anything else.

How Citizenship Changes This

Everything in this chapter - the role reversal, the expensive pile, the bridge years, the team you build - exists because your parent is a permanent resident rather than a citizen. Citizenship does not make the aging easier, and it does not open the envelopes for you. It does remove an entire layer of the difficulty. The five-year clocks stop mattering, sponsor deeming ends, public-charge worry disappears, and your parent gains access to the full safety net on the same terms as anyone born here. As you read on, you will see that nearly every hard problem in this book has the same ultimate solution written quietly underneath it. We will name it when it counts. For now, know that the destination has a name, and the journey toward it starts with the pile on the kitchen table.

PART ONE · BEFORE YOU BEGIN

CHAPTER 2

Why the Standard Advice Fails Your Family

The Seminar That Wasn't for Them

David almost didn't take his father to the free Medicare seminar. The flyer at the library looked reassuring. Coffee, a friendly-looking presenter, "Everything You Need to Know About Turning 65." His father, Mr. Chen, had insisted he was fine, that they didn't need to make a fuss.

They sat in the third row. The presenter was warm and clear. She explained that Part A is free "because you've paid into it your whole working life." She said that everyone should enroll "in the three months before your 65th birthday." She talked about penalties, about choosing between Original Medicare and Advantage plans, about signing up online in "just fifteen minutes."

David watched his father nod along politely, the way he nodded at things he didn't fully follow. David felt a slow, sinking realization. His father had come to the United States at 61, to be near the grandchildren. He had worked most of his life in Taiwan, not here. He had a green card, not citizenship. He had maybe two years of U.S. work credits, not forty.

Almost nothing the presenter said actually applied to Mr. Chen. Part A would not be free for him. The "fifteen minutes online" would run into a wall. And a rule the presenter never mentioned, one about five years of residence, was quietly ticking in the background of his father's life, and no one in that room had said a word about it.

They left with the same coffee everyone else got and a folder of glossy brochures that answered questions Mr. Chen didn't have and ignored every question he did. On the drive home, his father was quiet. "It was good," he finally said. That was the polite verdict he gave to things that had made him feel out of place. David didn't correct him. He understood, for the first time, that the problem was not his father. The problem was that the whole room had been built for someone else.

If you have ever sat in a room like that, or read a Medicare article that seemed to be describing someone else's parents, this chapter is for you. The advice is not wrong, just simply not written for your family, and the gap between the two is exactly where families lose money.

Four Hidden Assumptions

Almost every piece of mainstream Medicare guidance rests on four assumptions that are invisible to the people who write it, because for most Americans they are simply true. For your parents, one or more of them is false, and each false assumption is a place where the standard advice quietly breaks.

Assumption 1: The reader is a U.S. citizen. This is the deepest and most invisible assumption of all. Citizenship is treated as the water everyone swims in, so no one mentions it. But the entire benefits system treats citizens and non-citizens differently. A citizen turning 65 has no residence requirement, no five-year welfare bar, no sponsor whose income counts against them, and no public-charge concern. A permanent resident has all four of these hanging over the same birthday. When a guide says "at 65, you simply enroll," it is describing a citizen's experience. Your parent's experience has extra doors, extra locks, and extra keys, and the standard guide hands you none of them.

Assumption 2: The reader has 40 U.S. work credits. "Part A is free" is the most repeated sentence in all of Medicare education, and it is true only for people who, or whose spouse, worked and paid Medicare taxes in the U.S. for about ten years, which is 40 credits. Many immigrant parents arrived in their 50s or 60s and never came close. For them, Part A is not free. It carries a monthly premium that, in 2026, runs $311 a month for those with 30 to 39 credits and $565 a month for those with fewer than 30, up to $6,780 a year for a benefit their neighbors get for nothing. A guide that says "free" is not lying to your family so much as forgetting it exists.

Consider what this actually means in dollars. Take Mr. Chen from the seminar. With only about two years of U.S. work, roughly 8 credits, well under 30, he falls into the highest premium tier: $565 a month in 2026, or $6,780 a year, just for Part A. His neighbor, a retired citizen with a full work history, pays $0 for the identical coverage. If Mr. Chen lives another twenty years, that gap alone is more than $135,000, not counting Part B, not counting any penalty, not counting inflation. The seminar presenter, standing in front of both of them, quoted the same "free" to the whole room. For one man it was true. For the other it was a six-figure error, delivered with a smile.

The good news is that this cost is often reducible. Chapter 9 shows the legitimate ways to build toward those credits, through a spouse's record, an ex-spouse's record after a long marriage, or a late-career job taken to reach the finish line. A parent sitting at 32 credits, for instance, may need only two more years of modest work to move from a premium tier all the way to premium-free coverage. The point for now is this: never accept "Part A is free" as true for your family until you have counted your parent's credits.

Assumption 3: The reader is comfortable with English. The standard advice assumes you can read a dense enrollment notice, follow a phone tree, compare plan documents, and catch the fine print. Your parent may do well in daily life and still be unable to safely navigate a Medicare Summary Notice or a Part D formulary, documents that challenge native English speakers. This is not about intelligence, but rather about specialized vocabulary in a second language, under time pressure, with money on the line. The "fifteen minutes online" assumes a reader who is not your parent. In practice, this assumption is why the letters end up in the quiet pile, and why the work so often lands on you.

Assumption 4: There is no sponsor and no clock. Mainstream guidance never mentions the affidavit of support (Form I-864) that a family sponsor signed to bring your parent here, because most readers do not have one. But that affidavit can cause the sponsor's income to be "deemed" available to your parent, which can block need-based help like SSI (Supplemental Security Income) and Medicaid for years. Nor does the standard guide mention the five-year clocks that govern when a permanent resident can access certain benefits. These are the main event, not footnotes for your family. A guide that ignores them is not merely incomplete. For your parent, it is pointed in the wrong direction.

The Four Structural Challenges

The hidden assumptions explain why the advice is wrong for your family. There is a second layer. Even when the right information exists, four structural forces make it harder for immigrant families to find it, trust it, and act on it. These are not personal failings, but mere features of the landscape, and naming them helps you plan around them.

The first challenge is language access. The most important benefits documents in your parent's life arrive in dense English, and the systems behind them are only patchily translated. Medicare and Social Security offer some materials and interpreter lines in other languages, but coverage is uneven, the specialized vocabulary rarely translates cleanly, and the highest-stakes notices are often English-only. This is why so much falls to the adult child. You become the translation layer the system assumes already exists. Plan for this by never letting your parent face a consequential document alone, and by knowing that free interpreter help is available on the official phone lines, 1-800-MEDICARE and Social Security's 1-800-772-1213, even when the paperwork is not translated.

The second challenge is community misinformation. In tight-knit immigrant communities, information travels fast and warmly, from a friend at church, a relative, a familiar face on WeChat, KakaoTalk, or WhatsApp. That closeness is a gift, but it also means a single wrong belief can spread and harden into "everybody knows." Picture a Saturday gathering where an aunt announces, with total confidence, that her friend's husband applied for a low-income drug subsidy and then had his green-card renewal delayed, so whatever you do, do not sign your mother up for any of those programs. By Monday, three families have quietly decided to skip benefits their parents had fully earned, over a story that was secondhand, incomplete, and almost certainly about something else entirely. That is how a single warm, well-meant sentence costs several families thousands of dollars each. Two myths do the most damage. The first is that using any benefit will endanger a green card, which it usually will not, as shown in Chapter 7 on public charge. The second is that Part A is free for everyone, which it is not, for many immigrant parents. Treat community wisdom as a lead to verify, not a conclusion to act on.

The third challenge is a shortage of immigrant-aware advisors. Most Medicare agents, financial planners, and even benefits counselors rarely encounter clients with sponsor deeming, totalization, or five-year clocks, so they simply do not think to ask about them. An advisor can be skilled, honest, and completely unequipped for your parent's situation, and you may not discover the gap until a mistake is made. This scarcity is exactly why Chapter 19 is devoted to vetting for immigrant experience specifically, rather than just credentials. The right questions to ask are: "are you licensed?" and "have you worked with non-citizen clients, and do you understand the five-year rules?"

The fourth challenge is cultural decision-making differences. Mainstream advice assumes an individual, self-directed senior who researches options and enrolls online. Many immigrant families make these decisions differently, collectively, with adult children leading, and often with a cultural instinct toward stoicism. "I don't want to be a burden." "We handle our own problems." "Don't make trouble." That instinct, admirable as it is, can delay action until a deadline has passed or discourage a parent from claiming help they have fully earned. Recognizing this pattern in your own family lets you gently reframe. Enrolling on time and claiming earned benefits is just using a system your parent has every right to use.

Why the Stakes Are Higher for Late-Life Immigrants

Every senior faces Medicare decisions. A parent who immigrated late in life is playing the same game with fewer chips and a shorter clock, and the reasons compound one another.

They arrived with fewer U.S. work credits, so premium-free Part A, the foundation everyone else takes for granted, is often out of reach, turning a free benefit into a bill of thousands of dollars a year. They have fewer years to build those credits before 65, so the usual fixes have less room to work. They are more likely to have a sponsor whose income is deemed against them, blocking the need-based programs that would otherwise cushion a low income. And they face the five-year clocks and public-charge questions that simply do not exist for citizens, extra obstacles arriving at the exact stage of life when energy for bureaucratic battles is lowest.

To see how these compound, imagine two neighbors turning 65 the same month. One is a lifelong citizen. The other is a permanent resident who came to the United States at 62, just three years earlier, at his son's invitation. The citizen pays $0 for Part A, and if her income is low enough, she can immediately claim a Medicare Savings Program to cover her Part B premium. The permanent resident pays $565 a month for Part A, is blocked from that same Savings Program by the five-year bar, and has his sponsor's income counted against him besides. Same birthday, same town, same health. But by the end of year one, the gap between them can already exceed $8,000, and it widens every year until credits or citizenship close it. Nothing about this is the resident's fault. It is simply the system working exactly as written, for a person the standard advice forgot.

Layer on top of this that late-life immigrants often have less retirement savings from U.S. employment, may be supporting or supported by adult children in a delicate financial balance, and frequently need long-term care within the very window when they are least eligible for the program, Medicaid LTSS (Long-Term Services and Supports), that would pay for it. The result is that a single missed deadline or wrong move costs a late-life immigrant family proportionally more than it would cost a citizen family. The penalties are the same size, but they land on a smaller foundation.

This is why the careful, early planning this book describes matters so much for your family in particular. When the margin for error is this thin, the danger reaches beyond just missing information into confidently wrong information, delivered in the voice of authority by a seminar, a brochure, or a neighbor who genuinely means well. So this book's first job is to replace confident-but-wrong guidance with guidance built for your actual situation. It all comes back to one question you can ask of any advice you are given. Does this assume my parent is a citizen with a full U.S. work history? If it does, it may not be for your family, and now you will know to look deeper.

Action Checklist

- ☐ Audit your current sources. List where your family's Medicare information is coming from, whether a seminar, a brochure, a relative, or a community chat group. For each, ask whether it assumes citizenship and 40 U.S. credits.
- ☐ Write down your parent's four facts. Record status (citizen or LPR, Lawful Permanent Resident), rough number of U.S. work credits, English comfort with official documents, and whether anyone signed an I-864 to sponsor them. These four facts determine which advice applies.
- ☐ Flag the "free Part A" assumption. If your parent has fewer than 40 U.S. credits, mentally cross out every "Part A is free" statement you encounter until you have read Chapter 9.
- ☐ Name your language plan. Decide who reads consequential documents with your parent, and note the free interpreter lines, 1-800-MEDICARE and Social Security's 1-800-772-1213, for the moments you need them.
- ☐ Screen community advice through the four facts. When a relative or chat group shares a "rule," write it down as a question to verify, not a decision, and check it against your parent's situation.
- ☐ Talk about the "burden" instinct out loud. If your family tends toward stoicism, name it gently and reframe. Enrolling on time and claiming earned benefits is using a right, not asking for charity.

- ☐ Find one immigrant-aware resource. Bookmark your State Health Insurance Assistance Program (SHIP), which offers free, unbiased counseling and is used to non-citizen questions. You will build the rest of the team in Chapter 19.

How Citizenship Changes This

This chapter is, in a sense, entirely about citizenship, because three of the four hidden assumptions, status, the sponsor, and the clocks, exist only for non-citizens, and they drive much of what makes the stakes higher for late-life immigrants. For a citizen, the standard advice mostly works. No residence requirement, no deeming, no five-year bar, no public-charge shadow. The moment your parent naturalizes, the ordinary Medicare guidance you find everywhere becomes reliable for them, and the structural challenges shrink to the ones any family faces, chiefly language. To put it another way, naturalization does not just add benefits. It makes the whole world of ordinary advice finally apply to your parent. That is a quieter benefit than the dollars, but for a family tired of feeling like the exception, it may be one of the most valuable.

Part One · Before You Begin

Chapter 3

What's Actually at Stake

"It's Not a Parking Ticket"

"You're still putting off your mom's Medicare thing?"

Adrienne didn't look up from her coffee. "It's on the list, Priya. It's a long list."

"Okay, but can I tell you what my brother learned the hard way?" Priya leaned in. "These mistakes aren't like a parking ticket. Some of them follow you forever."

"Forever how?"

"My dad enrolled late. Nobody told him the window mattered. Now he pays extra on his premium every single month, and he'll pay it for the rest of his life. It never goes away."

Adrienne finally looked up. "Wait. For the rest of his life? For being late once?"

"For being late once."

That night, Adrienne sat down with a calculator and a legal pad, despite not being a numbers person. She started adding it up anyway. A late penalty here. A Part A premium there. A benefit her mother might qualify for but had never claimed. Her rough, conservative math frightened her. The total was not a parking ticket. It was a used car. Then a down payment. Then, in the worst version, a small inheritance, gone. Lost, not to a person but to deadlines and rules no one had explained.

She didn't finish the list that night. She never called it "the Medicare thing" again. She started calling it what it was: the most expensive paperwork of her mother's life.

This chapter is Adrienne's legal pad. This isn't here to scare you. It's here to make the invisible visible, because you can't protect against a cost you can't see.

And once you can see it, nearly every dollar on this list is defendable.

The Five Leaks

Money does not drain out of an immigrant senior's finances all at once. It leaks slowly and quietly, through five specific gaps. Any one of them can cost thousands. Together, over a retirement, they can reach the low-to-mid six figures. Let us name each one, because a named leak can be plugged. Under each, I have put a rough dollar figure so the abstract becomes concrete. These are not your family's exact numbers, but they show the scale.

Leak 1: Medicare late-enrollment penalties. These are the cruelest, because they are permanent. Miss your parent's Part B enrollment window without qualifying coverage, and Medicare adds 10% to the monthly premium for each full 12-month period they could have been enrolled but weren't, and that surcharge lasts for life. Part D carries its own lifetime penalty. A parent who delays Part B by three years could pay roughly 30% more, every month, for as long as they live. On the 2026 base premium of $202.90, that compounds across decades into thousands of dollars. This is Priya's father's leak, the one that "follows you forever." Chapters 13 and 14 show how to close it before it opens.

Leak 2: Part A premiums that did not have to be paid. For a parent without 40 U.S. work credits, Part A is not free. In 2026 it costs $311 a month with 30 to 39 credits, or $565 a month with fewer than 30, as much as $6,780 a year for coverage their neighbors get for nothing. Over a twenty-year retirement, that is a six-figure figure on its own. The leak here is not always avoidable, but it is often reducible, through a spouse's credits, a few more quarters of work, or the buy-in math in Chapter 9.

Leak 3: Long-term care your family paid for out of pocket. Medicare does not cover extended long-term care, and in 2026 the national median for a private nursing-home room runs about $129,575 a year. The program that does pay for it, Medicaid long-term services and supports (LTSS, Long-Term Services and Supports), is largely closed to permanent residents inside the five-year bar. A family that does not plan for this gap can watch a lifetime of savings disappear in two or three years of care. Chapter 17 confronts this directly.

Leak 4: Need-based benefits never claimed. Medicare Savings Programs, Part D Extra Help, and in some cases SSI (Supplemental Security Income) can be worth thousands of dollars a year. The 2026 SSI federal rate alone is $994 a month. Many immigrant families never apply, either because they do not know these exist, or because they fear it will endanger a green card. It usually will not, as shown in Chapter 7. Every year unclaimed is money left on the table that your parent had a right to.

Leak 5: Bridge-year coverage bought the expensive way. In the years before your parent qualifies for or can afford Medicare, families often overpay for coverage, buying a full-price plan when a subsidized one was available, or going uninsured and gambling on a medical bill that could reach tens of thousands. Chapter 11 lays out the affordable bridge options, including 2026 Marketplace subsidies and the H.R.1 changes that affect them.

Adrienne's Legal Pad: One Family's Total

Numbers on their own are easy to shrug off. So let us do what Adrienne did and walk one plausible family through the leaks and add them up. Meet the Okafors. Mrs. Okafor is a permanent resident who arrived at 61 with about 12 U.S. work credits. Her family, like most, did not know the rules going in. Not every leak applied to them, but the ones that did were expensive.

She missed her Part B window by two years, not realizing the deadline mattered, a lifetime penalty of about $40 a month, or roughly $10,000 over her retirement (Leak 1). With only 12 credits, she pays the full $565-a-month Part A premium. Over twenty years, that is more than $135,000 (Leak 2). At 74, by then a permanent resident for thirteen years, well past the five-year bar, she needs eighteen months of nursing-home care and would very likely have qualified for Medicaid to help cover it. But the family never applied, terrified that accepting long-term care at government expense would jeopardize her green card. That fear is not baseless the way it is for smaller programs. Long-term institutional care is one of the few benefits that can matter in a public-charge review, as shown in Chapter 7. In her situation it was very likely misplaced, and it cost the family about $190,000 out of pocket (Leak 3). The same fear kept them from ever claiming a Medicare Savings Program and Extra Help she plainly qualified for, roughly $2,500 a year unclaimed for eight years, about $20,000 (Leak 4).

Add it up: over $355,000. Not from bad luck. Not from anything Mrs. Okafor did wrong. From four leaks, none of which anyone ever named for the family, and most of which were preventable. That is the number that stops people cold at the kitchen table, exactly as it stopped Adrienne.

Why Seeing the Number Matters

"I ran the numbers," Adrienne told her brother Marcus on the phone the next morning. "For Mom. Worst case."

"How bad?"

"Bad enough that I stopped calling it paperwork."

There was a long pause. "So what do we do?"

"That's the thing," Adrienne said. "Almost all of it is fixable, but only if we start now. The penalties are the ones we can't undo, and those come from missing dates. The rest is about claiming what she's owed and getting her toward citizenship."

Marcus exhaled. "Okay. Send me the list. I'll take half."

That conversation, not the calculator, is the real point of this chapter. No two families lose the same amount, and that's not the point. What matters is showing you where the leaks are, so you can walk through your own house, find which taps are running, and hand that map to the people who can help you close them.

The difference between the Okafors' $355,000 and a family that loses almost nothing is rarely money or luck. It is information and timing. That is the whole thesis of this book.

The Master Key

Read back through the five leaks and you will notice something. The Part A premium is driven by work credits, not by status. A citizen without 40 credits pays it too. But the rest of the picture is different. The closed door to Medicaid LTSS, the blocked need-based benefits, and the shakier bridge-year options are all consequences of one thing. Your parent is a permanent resident, not a citizen.

This is why, throughout this book, we return again and again to a single idea. Citizenship is the master key. There are actually two ways status can start opening those doors. A full 40-credit work record, on its own, lifts the five-year Medicaid bar, but not the SSI wait, and it does not touch the rest of the picture. Citizenship does the rest. It removes the five-year bar, ends sponsor deeming, erases public-charge worry, and opens the full safety net, Medicaid, LTSS, SSI, and the Savings Programs, on the same terms as any citizen. It does not undo the permanent penalties, so timing still matters, and it does not create work credits out of nothing, so Part A may still cost something. But it is the one move that clears everything else at once. Two of the five leaks close or shrink dramatically the day your parent naturalizes, and a third eases, while Part A cost stays tied to work credits either way.

That is not a reason to wait five years and do nothing in the meantime. In fact, the opposite is true. The bridge years are when you plug the leaks you can plug now while marching toward the key that closes the rest. It does mean that everything in this book points, quietly, toward the same destination. When you feel overwhelmed by the pieces, remember there is one move that simplifies almost all of them.

Action Checklist

- ☐ Walk your own house. Go through the five leaks and mark each one as "applies to us," "might apply," or "doesn't apply." You are building your family's personal risk map.
- ☐ Estimate your three big variables. Write down your parent's status (citizen or LPR, Lawful Permanent Resident), rough U.S. work-credit count, and whether a sponsor signed an I-864. These drive four of the five leaks.
- ☐ Flag the permanent leaks first. Enrollment penalties (Leak 1) cannot be undone later, so put reading Chapters 13 and 14 near the top of your list.
- ☐ Do not skip the "unclaimed benefits" leak out of fear. Note any need-based program you have avoided because of green-card worry, and plan to check it against Chapter 7 before ruling it out.
- ☐ Name the destination. If your parent is not yet a citizen, write "citizenship" at the top of your family's plan. Chapter 5 helps you weigh it, and Chapter 22 helps you do it.

CHAPTER 4

Three Landmines to Avoid First

"Don't Sign Anything Yet"

"I'm going to knock it all out Saturday," Marcus said. "Medicare, and while I'm at it, SSI and Medicaid. Money's tight for Mom, so the sooner the better."

His cousin Lena worked at a community legal-aid office, and something in her went still. "Wait. Before you apply for anything. Who sponsored Auntie to come here?"

"I did. I signed the… the affidavit thing. Why?"

Lena was quiet for a second. "Marcus, that affidavit means your income can count as hers when she applies for need-based programs. If you file for SSI the wrong way, at best it gets denied. And if she applies for the wrong benefit at the wrong time, it could even come up later when she goes for citizenship."

"So I shouldn't apply?"

"I'm saying don't apply blind. There are about three things you need to understand first, or your efficient Saturday could cost her." She smiled.

"Slow down. In this system, moving fast in the wrong direction is the expensive move."

Marcus put the pen down. It was the smartest thing he did all year.

Marcus almost made a mistake that thousands of well-meaning adult children make. Acting quickly, out of love, before understanding the terrain. This chapter is the pause before the action. There are three landmines that can turn a helpful move into a costly one, and all three are invisible if you do not know to look. This chapter's job is only to help you recognize them and get the order of your first moves right. The detailed navigation of each one comes later, in its own chapter.

Landmine 1: Sponsor Deeming

When your parent immigrated through a family member, that sponsor almost certainly signed an Affidavit of Support (Form I-864), a legally binding promise to financially support the immigrant. Most families sign it, file it away, and never think about it again.

But that affidavit has a long tail. For need-based programs like SSI (Supplemental Security Income) and full Medicaid, the government can treat the sponsor's income and resources as if they were available to your parent, a rule called deeming. Even if the sponsor is not actually giving your parent a dime, that income can count against them and push them over the eligibility limit, blocking benefits they would otherwise receive.

The single thing to take from this chapter is that deeming exists and that it can quietly disqualify an application you were sure would succeed. That is why applying for SSI or Medicaid without understanding it can lead to a confusing denial. Don't allow this rule to make you give up on these benefits. Rather, use it to understand where your family stands before you apply. This is exactly what Lena caught for Marcus. How deeming is actually calculated, when it ends, and how to read the I-864 to find your family's obligation are all covered in Chapter 7.

Landmine 2: Public Charge

"Public charge" is one of the most misunderstood and most feared concepts in immigrant communities, and that fear does real damage. Many families avoid benefits their parent has fully earned because they are terrified it will endanger a green card or a future citizenship application.

Here is the grounding truth as of 2026. The public-charge test looks at a narrow set of things, chiefly cash assistance for income maintenance and long-term institutionalization at government expense. It does not count Medicare, most Medicaid, the Medicare Savings Programs, Part D Extra Help, or ordinary health coverage. In plain terms, using the health benefits this book is mostly about does not, under the current rule, make your parent a "public charge."

Two cautions to carry out of this chapter. First, a rule change was proposed in late 2025 that could broaden what counts, and its status should be verified before you make any decision. Second, public charge is genuinely complex where cash aid or institutional long-term care is involved, so those specific situations deserve professional advice. The goal here is to replace blanket fear with accurate, narrow caution, so your parent does not skip help they have earned over a myth. The full list of what counts, the history behind why this rule keeps changing, and what to do if your parent has already used a counted benefit are all in Chapter 7.

Landmine 3: The Two Five-Year Clocks

This is the landmine that catches even careful families, because most people do not realize there are two different five-year rules, and they are easy to confuse.

The first is a Medicare residence rule. A permanent resident who does not qualify on a work record generally must have lived in the U.S. continuously as an LPR for the five years immediately before applying to buy into Medicare. Notice how this one works. It looks backward five years from the day your parent applies, and it disappears entirely if your parent has 40 work credits. This rule governs access to Medicare itself for parents without enough credits.

The second is the PRWORA (Personal Responsibility and Work Opportunity Reconciliation Act) welfare bar, a five-year waiting period that runs forward from the date your parent became a qualified immigrant, which for most parents is the date they got their green card, before they can receive federally funded need-based programs like full Medicaid and SSI. This rule governs access to the safety net.

For now, the only thing you need to hold is that these are two separate rules, not one. For a typical parent both are anchored to the same green-card date, so it is tempting to assume they are the same thing. But they gate different benefits, they are structured differently, with one a backward look-back at the moment you apply and the other a forward waiting period, and they are bypassed in different ways. Treating them as a single rule is how families expect help that is not available yet, or overlook help that is. Here is the throughline that runs under both, and under Landmine 1. Work credits and citizenship each open different combinations of these locks, and citizenship is the only key that opens all of them. Exactly how each is counted and bypassed is decoded side by side in Chapter 6.

How the Three Landmines Interact

Each landmine is dangerous on its own. The reason they belong together in one chapter, before any of them gets its own deep chapter, is that they rarely detonate one at a time. They compound, and the compounding is invisible if you only ever study them separately.

Start with the most common chain. A family sees that money is tight and rushes to apply for SSI, the natural, loving instinct. Sponsor deeming (Landmine 1) causes the application to be denied because the sponsor's income counts. So far, only time is lost. Now imagine the same family, in a different state or situation, successfully obtains a benefit that happens to be one of the narrow categories that matters for public charge (Landmine 2), applied for at a delicate moment, such as shortly before a citizenship interview. What began as a well-meant SSI application has quietly wandered into immigration-consequence territory. Two landmines, triggered by one hurried Saturday.

The two five-year rules (Landmine 3) sit underneath both of the others, setting the timing that makes them dangerous. Apply during the welfare-bar window and the need-based application fails on eligibility grounds before deeming is even reached. Misread the Medicare residence rule and your parent either misses coverage they could have had or pays for coverage they did not need yet. Here is the hopeful part. The same levers that solve so much of this book each defuse more than one trap, though only one defuses all of them. Forty work credits end sponsor deeming and make the Medicare residence rule moot, and for Medicaid they can also lift the five-year bar for a parent with a full 40-quarter record. SSI is the stubborn exception. There, a parent generally needs both the 40 quarters and the five years to pass. Citizenship, by contrast, clears deeming, both five-year rules, and the SSI wait all at once. So a single strategic move can disarm several landmines, and the ultimate move disarms them all. That is the hidden good news buried in this chapter. The landmines compound, but so do the solutions.

This is why the order of your moves matters more than their speed. You are not just avoiding three separate mistakes. You are avoiding the chain reaction that links them.

The Right Sequence

"Okay," Marcus said, pen still down. "So if I'm not doing everything Saturday, what am I doing?"

"You're doing it in order," Lena said. "Fast is fine. Blind is not."

"Give me the order."

"First, gather facts, don't file applications. Find the I-864, figure out roughly how many work credits Auntie has, and write down the date she got her green card. That's an afternoon, and it tells us which landmines are even live for her."

"Then apply?"

"Then we figure out what each rule says for her specific dates. That tells us what she's eligible for and when. Only after that do we touch a need-based application, because now we'll know whether deeming or the bar will sink it. Medicare enrollment usually runs on its own timeline and has its own hard deadlines, so we protect those windows separately. That part we don't delay."

Marcus wrote it down. "Gather, check the rules, then apply. And Medicare on its own track."

"Right. And anything that touches cash aid or long-term care, or anything close to a citizenship filing, that's when we bring in someone who does this for a living, before we act, not after."

The sequence Lena gave Marcus is the whole practical lesson of this chapter. Understand your family's facts, read the rules, then act on the need-based programs, while protecting Medicare's separate deadlines throughout, and pausing for professional help at the two genuinely high-stakes moments. Every later chapter fills in one piece of this order. This chapter just makes sure you do not act out of sequence and set off the chain.

Where a Medicare Agent Helps

A good Medicare agent is invaluable for plan choice and enrollment timing. Still, the three landmines in this chapter sit partly outside an agent's lane, and knowing that boundary protects you. Before your parent enrolls, tell the agent the facts that change the picture: your parent's immigration status, rough U.S. work-credit count, and whether a sponsor signed an I-864. A strong, immigrant-experienced agent will use these to time enrollment correctly and flag the Medicare residence rule, the one part of this chapter squarely in their expertise. But be clear on the limits. An agent is licensed to help with insurance plans, not to determine SSI or Medicaid eligibility, interpret deeming, or give public-charge advice. Those questions belong to a SHIP (State Health Insurance Assistance Program) counselor, a benefits specialist, or an immigration attorney. The best agents know exactly where their expertise ends and will tell you so. If an agent brushes past your immigration questions or assures you that public charge "isn't a problem, just apply for everything," treat that as a signal to find one who understands your family's situation. Chapter 19 shows you how to build the full team.

Action Checklist

- ☐ Gather facts before filing anything. Locate the I-864, estimate your parent's work credits, and write down their green-card date. This afternoon of work tells you which landmines are live.
- ☐ Read the rules before need-based applications. Do not apply for SSI or full Medicaid until you know where your parent stands on the welfare bar. Applying blind risks a denial that is harder to fix later.
- ☐ Keep the two five-year rules straight. Record the green-card date, and note that the welfare bar runs forward from it while the Medicare residence rule looks backward from the day you apply. Do not merge them.
- ☐ Protect Medicare's deadlines on their own track. Enrollment windows do not wait for the rest of your planning, so keep them on a separate timeline and never miss one.
- ☐ Replace public-charge fear with the facts. Note which benefits you have avoided out of fear, and check them against Chapter 7. Most health benefits do not count.
- ☐ Pause for a professional at the two high-stakes moments. Anything involving cash aid or institutional long-term care, or any benefit application near a citizenship filing, warrants an immigration attorney or legal-aid review first.
- ☐ Verify the public-charge rule status. Because a change was proposed in late 2025, confirm the current rule on USCIS.gov or with an attorney before deciding.

CHAPTER 5

Citizenship vs. Green Card: The Real Cost-Benefit

"Why Would She Change Now?"

"My mother's had her green card for thirty years," Daniel said. "She's never had a problem. Why would we spend money and put her through a test now, at seventy-one?"

The benefits counselor didn't argue. She just asked a question. "Has she ever needed long-term care? A nursing home, home aides, anything like that?"

"No. She's healthy, thank God."

"And if she did need it, say, in five years, do you know how she'd pay for it?"

Daniel opened his mouth, then closed it. "I assumed Medicare. Or Medicaid, if it came to that."

"Medicare doesn't cover long stays," the counselor said gently. "And Medicaid, the program that does, treats a green-card holder differently than a citizen in some situations. Not always. But sometimes by a lot. That's the thing about the green card. It works right up until the day it doesn't, and by then the choice you could have made years earlier is off the table."

Daniel sat with that. "So you're saying she should naturalize."

"I'm saying you should run the numbers before you decide she shouldn't. That's different."

This chapter is about running those numbers. Not with slogans about what citizenship "means," but with the concrete question every family in this book eventually faces. For your parent, in your situation, is naturalizing worth the cost and effort, and if so, when? By the end you will have a framework, not an answer, because the right answer genuinely differs from family to family.

What the Green Card Still Costs You

A green card is permanent in name, but it comes with four quiet limits that a U.S. passport does not. You have met all four already in earlier chapters. Here they are side by side, because the decision in this chapter turns on them.

First, the five-year Medicaid bar. Most permanent residents must wait five years from the date they got their green card before they can receive full, federally funded Medicaid, including the long-term-care coverage Medicare does not provide. There is one important exception, which we will return to below. A parent with a full 40-quarter U.S. work record can clear that Medicaid bar without naturalizing. Most late-arriving parents do not have those 40 quarters, which is why citizenship matters so much for them.

Second, sponsor deeming. If someone signed an Affidavit of Support (Form I-864) to bring your parent to the United States, that sponsor's income can be counted as if it were your parent's when they apply for need-based programs, often disqualifying them. Deeming ends at 40 work credits, at the sponsor's death, or at citizenship.

Third, public-charge exposure. As covered in Chapter 4 and detailed in Chapter 7, the public-charge test is narrow today, and most health programs do not count against a green-card holder. But the exposure exists, it creates fear that keeps families from claiming benefits they are entitled to, and the rules can tighten. A proposal to broaden the test was pending in late 2025. A citizen has no public-charge exposure at all. It is simply not a category that applies to them.

Fourth, the green card itself can be lost. It must be renewed, it can be abandoned through long absences abroad, and in rare cases it can be revoked. Citizenship, once granted, is permanent in a way a green card never is.

What Citizenship Removes, and What It Doesn't

Here is the honest ledger, because overselling citizenship would be as unhelpful as ignoring it.

Citizenship removes three of those four limits outright and clears the fourth. The five-year Medicaid bar disappears. Sponsor deeming ends. Public-charge exposure vanishes. And the green card's fragility becomes irrelevant, because there is no card left to lose. For a low-income parent who may someday need the safety net, Medicaid, long-term services and supports, SSI, and the Medicare Savings Programs, citizenship is what puts them on the same footing as any other American.

But citizenship does not do two things, and families who expect it to are disappointed. It does not make Part A free. Part A cost is tied to work credits, not to your passport. A citizen with fewer than 40 credits pays the same premium your permanent-resident parent would. And it does not erase Medicare's late-enrollment penalties, which are permanent once incurred and follow the person regardless of status. Those two leaks are governed by credits and calendars, not by citizenship.

Naturalizing opens the need-based safety net, Medicaid, LTSS, SSI, and Medicare Savings Programs, on citizen terms. It does not lower Part A premiums, which are set by work credits, and it does not undo enrollment penalties, which are set by timing. Weigh citizenship for the safety net, not for the premium.

The 40-Credit Wrinkle, and Why It Rarely Settles the Question

Some families ask a fair question. If 40 work credits can lift the Medicaid bar, why bother with citizenship at all?

Because 40 credits do less than citizenship does. A full 40-quarter record ends sponsor deeming, clears the five-year Medicaid bar, and makes the Medicare residence rule moot. But it does not, on its own, satisfy SSI, which generally requires both the 40 quarters and a five-year wait. It does not remove public-charge exposure. And it does not give your parent the permanence and simplicity of a passport. Citizenship does all of that at once. So for most families the 40-credit path is a strong partial bridge, useful when it applies, while citizenship remains the destination. The exception is the parent who already has a long U.S. work history and no interest in the test. For them, the credits may do enough. That is a real case, just not the common one.

What Citizenship Costs, in Dollars and in Effort

The dollar cost of naturalizing is a filing fee plus, for some families, the cost of help preparing the application. As this book goes to print, the Form N-400 fee is $760 to file by mail or $710 to file online. Lower-income families have two forms of relief, and it is worth knowing which one applies. If your parent's household income is at or below 150% of the Federal Poverty Guidelines, they may qualify for a full fee waiver (Form I-912) and pay nothing. If their household income is above 150% but no more than 400% of the Federal Poverty Guidelines, they may instead qualify for the reduced fee of $380 (Form I-942). For a family of four in 2026, that upper limit for the reduced fee is about $132,000 a year, which is why more families qualify for help than expect to.

One caution to look out for: filing fees change, and a significant increase to the N-400 fee, along with proposed limits on fee waivers, was under consideration as this book went to press. Do not rely on the numbers printed here. Before your parent files, check the current fee on the USCIS Fee Schedule at uscis.gov or confirm it with a nonprofit immigration-services organization. This is a place where a printed figure can be out of date within months.

The effort cost is the application itself, the biometrics appointment, the interview, and, for many applicants, the English and civics tests. For an older parent, the tests are often the real worry, not the fee. That worry is frequently misplaced, as the next section explains.

The Senior Exemptions Most Families Don't Know About

The naturalization tests bend for older, long-resident immigrants. Three rules matter, yet many families have never heard of them.

The "50/20" rule applies to a parent who is age 50 or older and has lived in the United States as a permanent resident for at least 20 years. That parent is exempt from the English portion. They may take the civics test in their own language, with an interpreter.

The "55/15" rule applies to a parent who is age 55 or older with at least 15 years as a permanent resident. That parent gets the same English exemption, civics in their own language, with an interpreter.

The "65/20" accommodation applies to a parent who is age 65 or older with at least 20 years as a permanent resident. That parent not only takes civics in their own language, but studies a reduced set of civics questions written for older applicants.

For a parent who arrived decades ago and has always feared the English test, these rules can turn "impossible" into "manageable." And a parent with a disability that prevents them from meeting the test requirements may qualify for a medical exception (Form N-648). The point is simple. Do not rule out citizenship because you assume your parent cannot pass a test in English. Many do not have to take it in English at all.

The Decision Framework

Put it together, and the decision comes down to three questions, weighed honestly for your own family.

First, timing. How close is your parent to the safety net they might need? A healthy sixty-five-year-old with savings has time to plan. A frailer parent, or one already inside a five-year bar with no 40-quarter record, has more urgency. Citizenship takes time to obtain, so the further ahead you start, the more it can protect.

Second, likelihood of needing the net. Be honest about income, health, and family support. A parent who will almost certainly need Medicaid long-term care someday has far more to gain from naturalizing than one who is comfortably provided for. Citizenship's biggest payoff is precisely in the situations families least like to imagine.

Third, cost and difficulty for this parent. Between the reduced fee, the fee waiver, and the senior test exemptions, the real cost for a low-income, long-resident parent is often far lower than families assume. Price it out with the current fee and the exemptions your parent qualifies for before you conclude it is too expensive or too hard.

There is no universal answer. A well-off parent with strong family support and 40 work credits may reasonably stay a permanent resident. A lower-income parent who may one day need long-term care almost always benefits from naturalizing, and usually sooner than the family first thinks. This chapter's job is to make sure the decision is made with the numbers in front of you, the way Daniel's family finally made it.

Action Checklist

- ☐ List your parent's four green-card limits. Decide which of the four, the Medicaid bar, deeming, public-charge exposure, or card fragility, actually apply to your family right now. That is your motivation, in concrete terms.
- ☐ Check the 40-credit question first. If your parent has or is near 40 work credits, note what that alone would unlock, which is ending deeming, clearing the Medicaid bar, and making the Medicare residence rule moot, and note what it would not unlock, which is SSI and public charge. Chapter 9 helps you count credits.

- ☐ Price citizenship honestly. Look up the current N-400 fee on uscis.gov, do not trust a printed figure, and check whether your parent qualifies for the reduced fee or a fee waiver.
- ☐ Match your parent to a test exemption. Run their age and years as a permanent resident against the 50/20, 55/15, and 65/20 rules before assuming the tests are a barrier.
- ☐ Weigh the three questions. Consider timing, likelihood of needing the safety net, and cost and difficulty for this parent, and write down where your family lands on each.
- ☐ If citizenship is the answer, put it on the calendar. Chapter 22 walks through the application step by step. The best time to start is almost always earlier than it feels.

CHAPTER 6

The Two Five-Year Clocks, Decoded

"But It's the Same Five Years, Right?"

[illegible]

[illegible]

[illegible]

[illegible]

The Two Five-Year Clocks, Decoded

"But It's the Same Five Years, Right?"

Rosa had done her homework, which was why she was confused.

"I read that my father has to wait five years for Medicaid," she told the counselor. "And I read that he needs five years of residence for Medicare. So it's the same five years, and once it's up, he's covered for both."

"They're two different rules," the counselor said. "They often start on the same day, so people assume they're one thing. But they measure different situations, they're counted in opposite directions, and your father may not have to satisfy one of them at all."

"Opposite directions?"

"One looks backward from the day he applies for Medicare. The other counts forward from the day he got his green card. And if he has enough U.S. work credits, the first rule stops applying to him, and the Medicaid side of the second one lifts as well. Only SSI would still make him wait the full five years."

Rosa took notes for the rest of the meeting. This chapter covers what she learned, so you can place your own parent's dates against each rule and know exactly where they stand.

Why the Two Rules Get Confused

The confusion has a simple cause. Both rules use the number five, both involve immigration status, and for most family-sponsored parents, both begin on the same date, the day the green card was issued. They feel like a single waiting period.

They are two separate rules from two separate laws, and they do two separate jobs. Confusing them leads families to plan around a date that turns out to be wrong. The rest of this chapter separates them, explains how each is counted, and shows how work credits and citizenship change each one.

Rule A: The Medicare Residence Rule

This rule determines whether a parent can enroll in Medicare when they do not qualify through work.

Most people qualify for Medicare through their work record, meaning 40 credits of Medicare-taxed employment, either their own or a spouse's. A parent with that record is not affected by this rule. A parent without enough credits can still buy into Medicare, and that is where the residence rule applies. To enroll this way, the parent must be a lawful permanent resident who has resided continuously in the United States for the five years immediately preceding the application.

This is a backward-looking test. On the day the parent applies, Social Security looks back over the previous five years and asks whether the parent was a green-card holder living in the United States for that entire period. This is a condition measured at the moment of application. A parent who has been a permanent resident for six years satisfies it. A parent who received a green card two years ago does not yet satisfy it.

A parent with 40 work credits is exempt from this rule entirely. Reaching a full 40-quarter record allows enrollment through the work record, and the residence requirement never applies. This is one of the main reasons the credit count in Chapter 9 matters.

What "Continuous" Means, and What Breaks It

The critical word in this rule is continuous. Five years of U.S. residence is not the same as five years spent in the country at various times. The residence must run without a significant break for the five years immediately before the parent applies, and a long absence can break it and reset the count to zero.

Short trips do not break continuous residence. Social Security permits temporary absences, such as a vacation or a family visit lasting a few weeks, as long as the parent maintains a permanent home in the United States. A parent who travels to their home country for six weeks each year and then returns to the residence where they live has not broken their continuous residence, and the five years continue to accrue.

A long absence is treated differently. Once an absence exceeds six months, Social Security examines whether the parent intended to keep living in the United States or had relocated abroad. If the agency determines that U.S. residence was broken, a new five-year period begins on the date the parent returns to the United States. The earlier years no longer count toward the requirement.

This produces a common and expensive misunderstanding, because a parent who has lived in the country for more than five years in total assumes the requirement is met. Consider Mr. Haddad. He received his green card and lived in the United States for four consecutive years. His mother then became ill in his home country, and he returned to care for her for a full year before coming back to the United States. He has lived in the United States for three consecutive years since returning.

Counted as total time, this appears to be seven years of U.S. residence, well beyond the five the rule requires. The rule does not count total time. Mr. Haddad's year abroad broke his continuous residence, and his five-year period restarted when he returned. The first four years no longer apply. Three years into his second period of residence, he is not yet eligible, and he needs two more years of continuous residence before he can enroll in Medicare through this rule.

The practical guidance is straightforward. A single long absence, often taken for compelling family reasons, can reset a five-year period the parent was relying on. If a parent has spent, or plans to spend, more than six months outside the United States, treat the residence requirement as an open question and confirm their standing before assuming they qualify. A parent with 40 work credits is exempt from this rule and does not need to track continuous residence at all. One caution for later. This rule governs enrolling in Medicare. The separate rules that can suspend SSI or Medicaid after a parent is already receiving them operate on a much shorter timeline and are covered in Chapter 18.

How to Confirm Where Your Parent Actually Stands

Before assuming your parent has met the five-year residence requirement, or worrying that a past trip ruined it, confirm the facts. Two records settle most questions, and both are available to families directly.

The first is the green card, which establishes when your parent became a lawful permanent resident. For a parent who has lived in the United States continuously since arriving, the residence start date is straightforward, and the five years run from that point.

The second record matters when there have been trips abroad. U.S. Customs and Border Protection maintains an official arrival and departure history for the past five years, available free at i94.cbp.dhs.gov. Entering your parent's name, date of birth, and passport information produces a dated list of every entry to and exit from the United States. This is the same category of record Social Security uses to evaluate continuous residence, so reviewing it in advance shows you what the agency will see. Print it and check whether any single absence exceeded six months. If none did, continuity is unlikely to be an issue. If one did, that trip is the one to examine closely.

There is a distinction Social Security draws that families should understand, because it prevents a common miscalculation. The five-year requirement is about residence, not mere presence. Residence means your parent's actual home was in the United States, demonstrated by real ties such as paying U.S. taxes, maintaining a home, holding a U.S. driver's license, and otherwise living here as a settled resident. Presence means only that the person was physically in the country. Short visits, even repeated ones, do not build residence. A parent cannot satisfy the five years by stringing together frequent trips while keeping their real home abroad.

The rule requires an enduring attachment to the United States for the full five years.

This distinction cuts both ways, and understanding it is what lets a family answer their own question. A parent who kept a genuine home in the United States and took ordinary trips remains a continuous resident, and short absences do not threaten that. A parent whose absence stretched past six months should be prepared to show that their home remained in the United States during the trip. If that evidence is strong, a long trip may not break continuity despite exceeding six months. If it is thin, the agency is more likely to treat residence as broken and restart the five years from the return date.

Working the numbers is then simple. Identify the residence start date, either the original one or, if a long absence broke continuity, the date of return. Count forward five years. If that point has passed and your parent maintained a genuine U.S. home throughout, the residence requirement is met. If it has not, the difference between that date and today is how much longer your parent must wait, unless they reach 40 work credits first, which removes the requirement entirely.

One point about timing. Social Security does not monitor a parent's residence or send warnings along the way. The residence question comes up only when your parent applies for Medicare, and if the records raise a question, the agency sends a written request for evidence before making any decision, giving the family a chance to respond. Because that response window is short, the documents that prove a maintained U.S. home should be gathered before applying, not after a letter arrives. What to keep on file, and how to respond if Social Security questions residence, are covered in Chapter 21.

Rule B: The PRWORA Welfare Bar

This rule determines something different, namely whether a parent can receive full, federally funded need-based benefits, primarily full Medicaid and SSI.

It comes from the 1996 welfare-reform law, PRWORA (Personal Responsibility and Work Opportunity Reconciliation Act), and it operates as a forward-counting waiting period. On the day the parent becomes a qualified immigrant, which for most parents is the day they receive their green card, a five-year period begins. Until that period ends, the parent generally cannot receive those federally funded need-based programs. When it ends, the bar lifts.

This is the opposite motion from Rule A. The welfare bar counts forward from a starting date, while the Medicare residence rule looks backward from the application date. This is why describing them as the same five years is inaccurate even when they begin on the same day.

One detail matters for every family. Emergency medical care is never subject to this bar, and any otherwise-eligible immigrant can receive emergency Medicaid regardless of the waiting period.

How Work Credits and Citizenship Change Each Rule

This is where families can act to change their parent's standing, and the details require precision because the two rules respond differently.

Forty work credits do three things. They exempt the parent from the Medicare residence rule, they lift the five-year Medicaid bar by placing the parent in Medicaid's mandatory-coverage category, and they end sponsor deeming. Forty credits do not, on their own, qualify a parent for SSI. SSI requires both the 40 quarters and completion of the five-year waiting period. Work credits are powerful, but they do not resolve every rule.

Citizenship resolves all of them at once. It removes the Medicare residence rule, lifts the welfare bar, satisfies the SSI waiting period, and ends deeming. Chapter 5 covered the full decision to naturalize. This chapter shows precisely which requirements citizenship eliminates.

Quick Reference

- Medicare residence rule: backward-looking. Waived by 40 credits or citizenship.
- Welfare bar for full Medicaid: forward-counting. Lifted by 40 credits, by completing the five years, or by citizenship.
- SSI: requires both 40 credits and the five-year wait. Citizenship satisfies it.
- Sponsor deeming: ends at 40 credits, at the sponsor's death, or at citizenship. Full details in Chapter 7.

One Family's Timeline, Year by Year

The rules become concrete when charted against real dates. Mr. Nguyen received his green card in March 2023 at age 63, sponsored by his daughter. He has no U.S. work credits of his own, and he has lived in the United States without interruption since arriving, so his continuous residence is not in question. The following timeline shows how the two rules apply across his first several years, and how they move in opposite directions.

March 2023, green card issued, age 63. Both rules are now in effect, anchored to this date. The welfare-bar period begins counting forward. The Medicare residence rule will reference this date as the start of his continuous residence.

2025, age 65, Medicare age reached. This is the year the gap appears. Mr. Nguyen is eligible for Medicare by age, but the residence rule is not satisfied. Counting back five years from a 2025 application, he has been a permanent resident only since 2023, roughly two years. He does not pass the residence rule, and without work credits he cannot enroll through a work record. The welfare bar is also still running, two years into five, so full Medicaid is not available. He is old enough for Medicare but has not yet been a resident long enough to buy in.

2028, age 66, five years after the green card. Both five-year periods are now complete. Counting back from a 2028 application, he has been a continuously resident permanent resident for five years, so he passes the residence rule and can enroll. Five years have also elapsed forward from his 2023 green card, so the welfare bar has lifted and full Medicaid is available if he qualifies financially. For a parent with no work credits, this is the year his options open, and it arrives three years after he first became eligible by age.

SSI, throughout this period. SSI remains unavailable to Mr. Nguyen even in 2028, because it requires both the five-year wait, which he has now completed, and 40 work credits, which he does not have and, having arrived at 63, is unlikely to earn. This is why SSI is the hardest of these benefits to reach.

A single change alters the entire timeline. If Mr. Nguyen had arrived years earlier and built a full 40-quarter work record, the residence rule would not apply, the Medicaid bar would be lifted from the start, and deeming would end, leaving only the SSI waiting period. If he naturalizes at any point, every one of these requirements is resolved at once, including SSI. The dates are the same. Work credits and citizenship change the result.

The Trap Inside the Credit Count

One complication can affect the credit strategy, and it is narrow. It touches the forty-qualifying-quarter route for lifting the five-year Medicaid bar early. It does not touch premium-free Part A at all.

A quarter worked after December 31, 1996 does not count toward those 40 qualifying quarters if the parent received a federal means-tested benefit during that same quarter. The work still happened, and the earnings still appear on the record. Only the qualifying-quarter count for the Medicaid exemption is reduced. For most parents relying on their own work this rarely changes anything, because a parent who earned 40 quarters has usually lived here long enough to clear the five-year wait by time alone. It matters mainly in narrower cases, such as a parent trying to use the 40-quarter route to skip the wait early. Chapter 9 is where this count is worked out in full and kept separate from the Part A credit count, and it should be read before relying on any qualifying-quarter total.

A Rule Change on the Calendar

One change affects the welfare bar directly. A 2026 law commonly referenced as H.R.1 takes effect on October 1, 2026, and narrows federally funded Medicaid and CHIP eligibility for several immigrant categories. Beginning on that date, federal Medicaid and CHIP eligibility is limited primarily to lawful permanent residents, certain Cuban and Haitian entrants, and COFA migrants. For the lawful permanent residents this book addresses, the core structure described above still holds. Most permanent residents remain subject to the five-year waiting period, and the 40-quarter exemption remains in place.

The practical instruction is the one this book repeats throughout. Verify the current rule before acting. The information here is accurate as the book goes to press, but need-based eligibility for immigrants is an area of active legislative change. Confirm a parent's specific situation with a benefits counselor or the state Medicaid agency before making any decision that depends on it.

Action Checklist

- ☐ Record two dates: your parent's green-card issue date and the date they would apply for Medicare. Every calculation in this chapter depends on them.
- ☐ Pull your parent's travel history at i94.cbp.dhs.gov and confirm the residence start date before counting the five years. Check whether any single absence exceeded six months.
- ☐ Apply the Medicare residence rule (backward-looking): count back five years from the application date and confirm continuous permanent residence. If your parent has 40 credits, skip this rule.
- ☐ Account for any long absence over six months, which may reset the residence period to the return date. Short trips by a genuine U.S. resident do not count against your parent.
- ☐ Apply the welfare bar (forward-counting): count forward five years from the green-card date to see whether the full-Medicaid bar has lifted, or confirm that 40 credits have already lifted it.
- ☐ Treat SSI separately: it requires both 40 credits and the five-year wait.

- ☐ Review Chapter 9 before relying on any qualifying-quarter total, because benefits used while working after 1996 can reduce the 40-qualifying-quarter count for the Medicaid exemption. This affects only that exemption, never premium-free Part A.
- ☐ Verify current eligibility with a benefits counselor or state Medicaid agency before any status-dependent decision, given the October 1, 2026 changes.

PART TWO · STRATEGY 1: WIN ELIGIBILITY

CHAPTER 7

Sponsor Deeming and Public Charge

Two Landmines, Cleared

Chapter 4 named three landmines and told you to slow down before you tripped one. Two of those three belong to this chapter. Sponsor deeming can quietly disqualify a benefit application you were certain would succeed. Public charge can turn a well-meant application into an immigration problem, or, far more often, it can scare a family away from help their parent has fully earned. Both are misunderstood. Both are survivable once you understand how they actually work. This chapter takes them one at a time.

Part One: Sponsor Deeming

When your parent immigrated through a family member, that relative almost certainly signed an Affidavit of Support, Form I-864. It is a legally binding promise to support the immigrant financially, and the government treats it as real. For as long as the affidavit is in force, the sponsor's income and resources can be counted as if they were available to your parent when your parent applies for certain need-based programs. This counting is called deeming.

Deeming matters because it can block benefits even when no money changes hands. A parent living on almost nothing of their own can be treated, on paper, as having the sponsor's income, and denied on that basis. The programs affected are the federally funded need-based ones, chiefly SSI (Supplemental Security Income) and full Medicaid. Deeming does not touch Medicare. A parent's ability to enroll in Medicare, and the cost of their Part A premium, have nothing to do with a sponsor's income. This is worth saying plainly, because families often fear deeming will reach coverage it never touches. Deeming blocks the need-based layer around Medicare without blocking Medicare itself.

Deeming does not last forever. It ends when any one of four things happens. The parent naturalizes and becomes a U.S. citizen. The parent is credited with 40 qualifying work quarters, counting their own work and, in some cases, a spouse's. The parent permanently leaves the United States. Or the sponsor dies, which ends that sponsor's obligation. For a parent who arrived late in life with little prospect of earning 40 quarters, citizenship is usually the only realistic exit, which is one more reason the naturalization decision in Chapter 5 sits at the center of this book.

The forty-quarter exit deserves a word of caution, because it interacts with a rule covered in Chapter 9. Quarters worked after 1996 do not count toward the qualifying total for any quarter in which the parent received a federal means-tested benefit. The work still happened, and the earnings still show on the record, but the qualifying-quarter count for this purpose is reduced. This rarely changes the outcome for a parent relying on a long work history, but it can matter for a parent trying to reach the forty-quarter exit precisely to escape deeming. Chapter 9 works this out in full.

There is one relief valve worth knowing. It is called the indigence exception. If deeming would leave your parent unable to obtain food and shelter, an agency can, for a twelve-month period, count only the support the sponsor actually provides rather than the sponsor's full income. The exception must be requested; it is not automatic, and it can create a record that the sponsor was called on to support the immigrant, which carries its own consequences. It is a tool to raise with a benefits counselor or an attorney, not one to trigger casually. The mechanics of how deeming is calculated, and how to read the I-864 to find your family's specific obligation, are the kind of detail a SHIP counselor or legal-aid office can walk you through with the affidavit in front of you.

Part Two: Public Charge

Public charge is one of the most feared phrases in immigrant communities, and the fear does real damage. Families skip benefits their parent earned, avoid programs that would never count against them, and sometimes forgo care entirely, all over a rule most people have never seen described accurately. This section replaces the fear with the actual scope of the rule.

Start with what public charge can actually do, because that is what families are afraid of. Public charge is a ground of inadmissibility. A negative finding does not fine your parent or cut a benefit. It blocks a person at one of two doors. It can cause a green-card application to be denied for someone applying to become a permanent resident. And it can cause a person to be denied admission when they seek to enter or re-enter the country, which is the situation a current green-card holder can face after a long trip abroad. Underneath both of those is a quieter, more common harm. Because a past use of a counted benefit can be weighed in a future decision at either door, the rule frightens families into skipping benefits their parent had every right to use, including many that would never have counted. That avoidance is the way public charge hurts most of the families reading this book. It does not take anything away. It scares them out of claiming what was theirs.

Here is the grounding truth as of 2026. When the government decides whether someone is likely to become a public charge, it looks at a narrow set of things. Two benefit categories can count. The first is public cash assistance for income maintenance, such as SSI, TANF cash aid, and state or local general assistance paid in cash. The second is long-term institutionalization at government expense, such as a nursing-home or mental-institution stay paid by Medicaid.

Everything else in the health-benefits world is excluded. Medicare does not count. The Medicare Savings Programs do not count. Part D Extra Help, the Low-Income Subsidy, does not count. Ordinary Medicaid for health care does not count, and neither do home-based and community-based services that let a person receive care at home rather than in an institution. In plain terms, the health benefits this book spends most of its pages on are not public-charge benefits. Using them does not, under the current rule, make your parent a public charge.

The rule also does not apply to most of the people families worry about. It never applies to U.S. citizens, including the citizen children of immigrants. It generally does not apply to a permanent resident who already has a green card and is simply living their life, renewing the card, or applying to naturalize. Public charge is chiefly a test applied when someone seeks admission to the United States or applies to become a permanent resident. A parent who already holds a green card and is not leaving the country to seek readmission is, in the ordinary case, well outside the situations where the test is applied.

The one part of this that requires real care is long-term institutional care paid by Medicaid, because it is the single health-related item that can weigh in a public-charge analysis. Even there, it is considered within a totality of circumstances rather than as an automatic disqualifier, and home-based and community-based care is treated differently from institutional care. A family facing a nursing-home decision for a parent who is not yet secure in their status should get advice specific to their situation before acting. This is the narrow slice where the fear has a grain of truth, and Chapter 17 returns to the long-term-care question in full.

Two cautions close this section. First, public-charge rules have changed repeatedly with changes in administration, and a proposal to broaden what counts was pending in late 2025. Nothing in this chapter should be treated as settled without checking the current rule at uscis.gov or with an immigration attorney before you act. Second, the situations that genuinely carry risk, cash assistance and institutional long-term care are exactly the ones that deserve professional advice rather than a decision made at the kitchen table. The point isn't to make your family fearless, but to trade a blanket fear that costs families thousands in unclaimed benefits for a narrow, accurate caution aimed at the two things that actually matter.

How the Two Fit Together

Deeming and public charge are different rules that families blur into a single anxiety. Deeming is about eligibility. It can block a need-based application today because a sponsor's income counts. Public charge is about immigration status. It can matter when someone seeks admission or a green card, and for the health benefits in this book it usually does not apply at all. The practical lesson from both is the same one Chapter 4 opened with. Gather your facts, understand which rule is actually in play, and bring in a professional before acting on anything that touches cash assistance, institutional long-term care, or a pending immigration filing. Most of the time, once you see the rules clearly, the path is more open than the fear suggested.

Where a Medicare Agent Cannot Help

Neither deeming nor public charge is a Medicare agent's job, and a good agent will tell you so. An agent handles plan choice and enrollment timing, and those are unaffected by either rule, because deeming does not touch Medicare and public charge does not apply to ordinary coverage. What an agent should do is stay in their lane. If an agent tells you that using Medicare or a Medicare Savings Program will endanger your parent's green card, that is wrong, and it is a sign to find an agent who understands immigrant clients. Questions about SSI, full Medicaid, deeming, and public charge belong to a SHIP (State Health Insurance Assistance Program) counselor, a benefits specialist, or an immigration attorney. Chapter 19 shows you how to assemble that team.

Action Checklist

- ☐ Locate the Affidavit of Support, Form I-864, if a sponsor signed one. It defines who is bound and for how long, and it is the starting point for any deeming question.
- ☐ Remember that deeming never blocks Medicare. It can block SSI and full Medicaid, but a parent's Medicare enrollment and Part A premium are unaffected by a sponsor's income.
- ☐ Know the four ways deeming ends: the parent naturalizes, reaches 40 qualifying work quarters, permanently leaves the United States, or the sponsor dies. Identify which exit is realistic for your family.
- ☐ Ask about the indigence exception only with a counselor or attorney. It can help a parent who cannot otherwise obtain food and shelter, but it must be requested and can create a support record.

- ☐ Understand what public charge can do before you fear it: it can block a green-card application or an entry at the border, and it frightens families out of claiming benefits they had a right to. It cannot revoke citizenship or take away a green card your parent already holds while they remain in the country.
- ☐ Hold the public-charge rule to its narrow scope. Only cash assistance for income maintenance and long-term institutionalization at government expense can count. Medicare, the Savings Programs, Extra Help, ordinary Medicaid, and home-based care do not.
- ☐ Know who public charge never touches: U.S. citizens, and in the ordinary case, a permanent resident who already holds a green card and is not seeking readmission or a new status.
- ☐ Treat institutional long-term care as the one health item that can matter, and get advice specific to your parent before making a nursing-home decision that would be paid by Medicaid. Chapter 17 covers the long-term-care question in full.
- ☐ Verify the current public-charge rule at uscis.gov or with an immigration attorney before acting, because a change was proposed in late 2025 and the rule has shifted before.

A Note on Rules That Keep Moving

Immigration rules are not carved in stone. They shift with administrations, court decisions, and new guidance, and public charge is one of the rules that moves most. Here is a live example that was unfolding as this book went to print.

For years, only cash assistance for income maintenance and long-term care paid by the government at an institution were weighed in a public-charge decision. Programs like most Medicaid and SNAP did not count. Then, on July 20, 2026, the government announced it was removing the rule that set those limits, with the change scheduled to take effect September 18, 2026. Once in effect, officers could weigh a wider range of means-tested benefits, including Medicaid and food assistance, as part of a broader, case-by-case review. As this book went to print, the change was also expected to face legal challenges, which means its timing and its details could shift again.

I want you to know that keeping this book current is a promise I take seriously. I have worked to bring you the most up-to-date rules I possibly can, and when this change surfaced just before publication, I would not let it slip by unmentioned. You deserve nothing less than the freshest picture I am able to give you, even when the news arrives at the last possible moment.

Two things stayed true throughout, and they are worth holding onto. Public charge never changes whether your parent is eligible for a benefit; it only bears on certain green-card and admission decisions. It does not apply to U.S. citizens, and it is not part of the citizenship application, so a green-card holder who used benefits and then applies to naturalize is not judged on public charge in that step. For a parent who already holds a green card and stays in the country, it generally stays in the background. The main way it can resurface is a long trip abroad, more than about six months at a stretch, which can make a returning green-card holder be treated as seeking admission again. If your parent spends extended time in their home country, raise it with an accredited representative or elder-law attorney before they travel.

The lesson is not to memorize today's list. It is to check the rule before you act. Before your family relies on anything in this chapter, confirm the current public-charge policy at uscis.gov or with an accredited representative or elder-law attorney. A rule you looked up last year may not be the rule that applies this year. I did my part to keep this current; your part is to check it again when your moment comes.

Part Three · Strategy 2: Surviving the Bridge Years

Chapter 8

Which Parent Do You Have? Four Profiles

"My Situation Is Different"

Two sisters compared notes after each had read the same Medicare guide.

"It said my mother gets Part A for free," Elena said. "She worked here for thirty years."

"Mine said the opposite," Marisol answered. "My father came at sixty. The same book told me he'd pay almost seven thousand dollars a year."

"Same book. Same page, probably."

"Same page. Different fathers. Different rules."

Both sisters were right, and that is the point of this chapter. General Medicare advice fails immigrant families because it assumes one kind of parent. In reality there are several, and the differences between them decide almost everything: whether Part A is free, whether a five-year rule applies, how long the bridge to coverage lasts, and whether citizenship is urgent or optional. Before applying any strategy, you need to know which parent you have.

This chapter describes four profiles. Most parents fit one of them cleanly. Some fit two, usually because a situation is changing. Identify your parent's profile now, because the four chapters that follow build a plan around it.

The Four Facts That Decide the Profile

Four facts separate one profile from another. You gathered most of them while reading Chapters 5 and 6. Confirm them before continuing.

The first is U.S. work credits. Record your parent's own credits, and separately note whether a current, former, or deceased spouse holds 40 credits, because the two lead to different profiles. Your parent's own 40 credits define the Worker, while a spouse's record defines the Spouse-Credit Parent, and keeping them separate now prevents a misdiagnosis later. The second is age at arrival, because a parent who arrived young had time to build credits and residence, while a parent who arrived near retirement did not. The third is the green-card date, because both five-year rules are measured from it. The fourth is whether a sponsor signed an Affidavit of Support, because a sponsor's income can be deemed to the parent and can block need-based benefits. With these four facts in hand, the profile becomes clear.

Profile A: The Worker

The Worker is a parent who immigrated years ago, worked in the United States, and accumulated 40 or more work credits through their own employment.

This parent has the strongest position of the four. Part A is free because the credits are there. The Medicare residence rule does not apply, since 40 credits remove it. Sponsor deeming, if a sponsor ever signed, has ended because 40 credits end deeming. The five-year Medicaid bar is lifted as well, since a full credit record places the parent in the mandatory-coverage category. The only need-based program that still requires the five-year wait is SSI, and a parent with a long work record and other income often does not need it.

For the Worker, Medicare planning looks much like it does for a citizen. The work is in choosing coverage well and enrolling on time, not in overcoming eligibility barriers. Citizenship remains worthwhile for the permanence and the removal of public-charge exposure it provides, but it is not urgent for benefit access, because the credits have already opened most doors. Chapters 13 through 17 will matter more to this family than the bridge-year chapters.

Profile B: The Late Arrival

The Late Arrival is a parent who came to the United States near or after age 60, with few or no U.S. work credits, no qualifying spouse record, and often no realistic path to 40 credits of their own.

This parent faces the hardest version of every rule in the book. Part A is not free, and the premium can reach the highest bracket. The Medicare residence rule applies in full, so the parent cannot buy into Medicare until five continuous years of residence have passed. The welfare bar applies, so full Medicaid waits five years from the green-card date. SSI is effectively out of reach, because it requires both the five-year wait and 40 credits the parent will likely never earn. If a sponsor signed an Affidavit of Support, deeming compounds the problem, because 40 credits will not arrive to end it.

For the Late Arrival, citizenship is not optional planning because it is the single most powerful move available. After all, naturalization removes the residence rule, lifts the welfare bar, satisfies the SSI wait, and ends deeming all at once, none of which the parent can achieve through work. The bridge years are long and must be planned carefully, which is the work of Chapters 9 through 12. This is the profile the standard guides fail most completely, and the one this book was written for.

Profile C: The Sponsored Parent

The Sponsored Parent is a parent brought to the United States by an adult child or other relative who signed an Affidavit of Support, Form I-864. This profile often overlaps with the Late Arrival, but the sponsorship is the defining feature and deserves its own treatment.

The sponsorship creates a specific barrier that the other profiles may not face. Through deeming, the sponsor's income is counted as if it were the parent's when the parent applies for need-based programs such as SSI and full Medicaid. A parent with little or no income of their own can be treated as having the sponsor's income and denied on that basis, even though no money changed hands. Deeming continues until the parent reaches 40 work credits, the sponsor dies, or the parent naturalizes.

For the Sponsored Parent, the planning question is which of those three exits is realistic. A parent who arrived late is unlikely to reach 40 credits, which leaves citizenship as the practical route to ending deeming. Families in this profile should also understand that a sponsor can be asked to repay certain benefits the parent receives, which is one reason applications should not be filed without understanding deeming first. The full mechanics of deeming, including how it is calculated and how to read the I-864, are covered in Chapter 7.

Profile D: The Spouse-Credit Parent

The Spouse-Credit Parent is a parent who lacks 40 work credits of their own but is married to, divorced from, or widowed from someone who has them. Through a spouse's record, this parent can often reach premium-free Part A without ever having earned 40 credits alone.

This profile matters because it can move a parent who looks like a Late Arrival into a position close to the Worker. Premium-free Part A can be available on a spouse's record when the marriage meets the required length, and the other conditions are met. A current spouse's record can apply once the marriage has lasted at least one year and the working spouse is at least 62. A former spouse's record can apply after a marriage that lasted at least ten years, if the parent is now single. A deceased spouse's record can apply for a surviving spouse who was married at least nine months and is now single. The same spouse record that provides free Part A also removes the Medicare residence rule, because the parent then qualifies through work credits rather than through residence.

One caution matters at the profile stage, because it is the point families most often get wrong. When a parent reaches a full 40 quarters through a current or deceased spouse, those same quarters generally also lift the five-year Medicaid bar, so premium-free Part A and full-Medicaid eligibility tend to arrive together. Divorce is the exception. A ten-year former marriage can still provide premium-free Part A, but a former spouse's quarters generally stop counting toward the Medicaid bar once the marriage ends, so a divorced parent can have free Part A while still facing the five-year wait for full Medicaid. The rules that govern how spouse quarters are credited, and the precise conditions for current, divorced, and surviving spouses, are covered in Chapter 9.

When a Parent Fits Two Profiles

Some parents do not fit cleanly, and that is expected. A Sponsored Parent who arrived late is also a Late Arrival, and the two profiles reinforce each other, since both point toward citizenship as the decisive move. A parent who looks like a Late Arrival may turn out to be a Spouse-Credit Parent once a spouse's record is examined, which changes the plan substantially, because premium-free Part A and the removal of the residence rule come into reach.

When a parent fits two profiles, plan for the more demanding one first, then adjust as facts are confirmed. A family unsure whether a spouse's record will qualify should prepare as though it will not, while pursuing the confirmation that could improve the position. Planning for the harder case and being pleasantly corrected is safer than the reverse.

A Note on Self-Diagnosis

The four facts at the start of this chapter are enough to place most parents. Confirm your parent's own work credits through the Social Security earnings record, check whether a current, former, or deceased spouse holds 40 credits, confirm the green-card date from the card itself, confirm age at arrival from entry records, and confirm sponsorship by locating the I-864. If any of these is uncertain, treat the profile as provisional until the fact is verified, because an assumed credit total, an overlooked spouse record, or a missed sponsorship can send a family down the wrong plan.

What Your Profile Changes About the Agent Conversation

A Medicare agent helps with plan selection and enrollment timing, not with immigration status or need-based eligibility. Knowing your parent's profile tells the agent what to expect before enrollment.

• For the Worker, the conversation is a standard one about plan choice, because Part A is free and no residence rule applies.

• For the Late Arrival, the agent needs to know that Part A carries a premium and that enrollment may not be possible until the residence rule is met, which changes timing and cost.

• For the Sponsored Parent, the agent should understand that need-based help may be blocked by deeming, so the plan cannot assume access to those programs.

• For the Spouse-Credit Parent, tell the agent that premium-free Part A may be available through a spouse's record, since that changes both the cost and the enrollment path.

In every case, give the agent the profile up front so their recommendations rest on the parent's real situation rather than the standard assumptions.

Action Checklist

- ☐ Confirm the four facts: U.S. work credits (record your parent's own credits and any spouse's credits separately), age at arrival, green-card date, and whether a sponsor signed an I-864.
- ☐ Match your parent to one of the four profiles: Worker, Late Arrival, Sponsored Parent, or Spouse-Credit Parent.
- ☐ If your parent fits two profiles, plan for the more demanding one first and adjust as facts are confirmed.

- ☐ For a Worker, focus your reading on coverage choice and enrollment timing in Chapters 13 through 17.
- ☐ For a Late Arrival or Sponsored Parent, treat citizenship as the central strategy and read the bridge-year chapters, 9 through 12, closely.
- ☐ For a Spouse-Credit Parent, confirm with the Social Security Administration whether a current, former, or deceased spouse's record can provide premium-free Part A, and read Chapter 9 for how to claim it and how it affects the Medicaid bar.
- ☐ Give your parent's profile to any Medicare agent before discussing plans, so their advice reflects the real situation.

CHAPTER 9

Building Toward Premium-Free Part A

"I Thought Working Was Enough"

Wei sat at his kitchen table with two documents in front of him.

One was his mother's green card, issued in 2019 when she was sixty-one. The other was a printout from the Social Security website showing her earnings record.

"It says eighteen," he told his sister on the phone. "Eighteen credits."

"That can't be right. She worked."

"She worked. But the number says eighteen. Not forty."

Wei had assumed that because his mother worked, she had earned her way to free Medicare. The number told him otherwise. She was three years from sixty-five and less than halfway to the forty credits that make Part A free. His first reaction was to treat this as a wall. However, it is not a wall. It is a number, and numbers can be worked. This chapter shows how premium-free Part A is actually earned, how a spouse's record can deliver it, how to read the earnings statement that settles the question, and what it costs if the credits are not there. Chapter 8 told you which profile your parent fits. This chapter tells the Worker and the Spouse-Credit Parent how to confirm and finish the credit path, and it tells the Late Arrival and the Sponsored Parent what the premium will be if the credits never arrive.

What Forty Credits Actually Buys

Premium-free Part A is the goal because it removes the largest recurring cost an immigrant senior can face on the hospital side of Medicare. A parent with forty credits pays nothing for Part A for life.

Forty credits also does more than lower a premium. A full forty-quarter record lifts the five-year PRWORA (Personal Responsibility and Work Opportunity Reconciliation Act) Medicaid bar and ends sponsor deeming, as Chapter 6 explained. The one thing forty credits does not do on its own is satisfy SSI, which requires both the credits and the separate five-year wait. Chapter 6 laid out that split, and Chapter 18 covers the SSI mechanics in full.

Keep the two payoffs separate in your mind, because this chapter turns on the difference between them. Premium-free Part A is a Medicare rule, counted in quarters of coverage. The forty-qualifying-quarter Medicaid exemption is an immigration rule, counted differently. A parent can satisfy one and fall short on the other, and the rest of this chapter shows exactly when that happens.

How Credits Are Earned in 2026

Credits are earned through covered work, not through years lived in the United States. In 2026, a parent earns one credit for every $1,890 in covered earnings. Four credits is the annual maximum, which requires $7,560 in covered earnings for the year. A parent cannot earn more than four credits in a calendar year no matter how much they earn.

Forty credits equals ten years of covered work at the four-credits-per-year pace. A parent who works part of a year still earns credits for that year, up to the four-credit cap, as long as covered earnings reach the thresholds above.

This is why age at arrival matters so much. A parent who arrived at fifty-five with no prior U.S. work has a narrow window to reach forty credits before sixty-five. A parent who arrived at forty-five has room. Count the credits already earned, then count the working years left before the parent stops or before other paths become faster.

Reading the Earnings Statement

The document that settles the credit question is the Social Security earnings statement. It shows year-by-year covered earnings and the total credits earned.

Create or log in to a my Social Security account at ssa.gov to pull the statement, or request a certified itemized statement using Form SSA-7050 if you need the year-by-year detail. Read it in three passes.

First, find the total credit count. This is the number that determines premium-free Part A, and it tells you how far the parent is from forty quarters of coverage.

Second, check the year-by-year earnings against the annual thresholds. Confirm that years the parent believes they worked actually show covered earnings. Cash work and work not reported for Social Security taxes will not appear, and it does not count.

Third, if the parent is relying on the forty-quarter route to lift the Medicaid bar early, run the trap check described in the next section. This is a manual comparison the family does itself, because the statement shows quarters of coverage but never shows benefits received or disqualified quarters. This third pass affects only the Medicaid exemption count, not the Part A count from the first pass.

The result of these passes is two numbers, not one: the quarters of coverage that decide Part A, and the qualifying quarters that decide the Medicaid exemption. Build every later decision on whichever number the decision actually depends on.

The Post-1996 Quarter Trap

There is a rule that reduces one of those two numbers, and families miss it because the earnings statement does not flag it. The scope of this rule is narrow, so state it plainly before anything else. It reduces the forty-qualifying-quarter count used to lift the Medicaid bar early. It does not touch premium-free Part A.

A quarter worked after December 31, 1996 does not count toward the forty qualifying quarters for the Medicaid exemption if the parent received a federal means-tested benefit during that same quarter. There are five federal means-tested benefits: SSI, TANF, non-emergency Medicaid, SNAP, and CHIP. Emergency Medicaid is not on the list, so a quarter in which the parent received only emergency Medicaid is not disqualified.

Two points prevent the most common misreading. First, receiving one of these benefits does not erase the quarter for Part A. If the parent worked and paid Medicare taxes, the quarter still counts as a quarter of coverage toward premium-free Part A, no matter what benefits the household received. Second, being on Medicaid does not by itself void a parent's quarters. Only the specific quarters in which work and a means-tested benefit overlapped are disqualified, and only for the Medicaid exemption count.

For most parents relying on their own work, this trap rarely changes anything, because a parent who earned forty quarters has usually lived in the United States long enough to clear the five-year wait by time alone. It matters mainly in narrower cases, such as a parent using the forty-quarter route to lift the bar early before the five years have passed, or a spouse relying on the worker's quarters where the residence and work timelines do not line up. When one of those cases applies, match the work history against any period the worker received one of the five benefits, and subtract the overlapping post-1996 quarters from the exemption count.

One practical point matters here, because families expect to find this on a form and cannot. The Social Security earnings statement does not show disqualified quarters. It reports quarters of coverage from taxed work, and it never records or flags benefits received. Social Security does not track SNAP, TANF, Medicaid, SSI, or CHIP at all. The disqualification is applied later, by hand, by the state Medicaid or SNAP office when the family applies, using the family's own history of benefit receipt. That means the only way to know in advance is to do the comparison yourself. Take the years and quarters shown on the Social Security earnings record, then lay them against the periods the parent or the credited spouse received any of the five federal means-tested benefits after 1996. Any quarter where taxed work and one of those benefits overlap is a quarter the agency will not count toward the forty for the Medicaid exemption. Keep that list, because the family, not Social Security, is the only party holding both halves of the picture.

A Worked Count: The Ramirez Record

Tomás Ramirez arrived as a permanent resident in 2001 and worked in the United States for the next decade. His earnings statement shows 40 quarters of coverage. For premium-free Part A, that number settles it. Tomás has his 40 quarters, so his own Part A is free. The trap does not touch that number, and receiving any benefit along the way never would have.

The complication appears on the immigration side, and it appears through his wife. Rosa Ramirez joined Tomás in the United States last year as a permanent resident. Her health is poor, and she needs full Medicaid now. On her own, Rosa faces the five-year welfare bar because she has been a permanent resident for less than a year. The only way to lift that bar early is the 40-qualifying-quarter route, using Tomás's record while they are married.

This is where the trap bites. Tomás has 40 quarters of coverage, but in 2009 and 2010, during a stretch of unemployment, he received SNAP while picking up part-time work. Two of those post-1996 quarters overlapped a federal means-tested benefit. For the 40-qualifying-quarter Medicaid exemption, those two quarters do not count. Tomás has 40 quarters of coverage for Part A and only 38 qualifying quarters for the Medicaid exemption. Rosa is two short of the 40 she needs to lift her welfare bar early.

Note where the family found this out. Tomás's earnings statement showed a clean 40 quarters with no mark against the SNAP years, because Social Security does not record benefits. Rosa only learned she was short when she and Tomás sat down and matched his work record against the two years he had received SNAP. The agency would have reached the same result at application, but the family caught it first by doing the comparison themselves.

The consequence is concrete. Rosa cannot use Tomás's record to skip the wait, because his qualifying-quarter count falls to 38 once the two SNAP quarters drop out. She waits out the five-year bar, or the family looks at citizenship as the faster route for her. Tomás's own Part A is unaffected throughout, because the trap never reduces quarters of coverage. This is the point to carry forward. The same work record produces two different numbers, and the SNAP overlap that is invisible to Part A is exactly what keeps Rosa waiting.

A Spouse's Record Can Deliver Part A

A parent who never reaches forty credits alone can still get premium-free Part A through a spouse's work record. This is the Spouse-Credit Parent profile from Chapter 8. The rules differ by the parent's marital situation, and the 2026 conditions are specific.

A currently married parent qualifies for premium-free Part A on the spouse's record when the spouse has forty credits and is at least sixty-two. The marriage must have lasted at least one year before the parent applies.

A divorced parent qualifies on a former spouse's record when the marriage lasted at least ten years, the parent is now single, and the former spouse is eligible for Social Security benefits.

A widowed parent qualifies on a late spouse's record when the marriage lasted at least nine months before the spouse died and the parent is now single.

These are the general conditions, and exceptions exist. Confirm the parent's specific situation with Social Security at 800-772-1213 before treating spouse-based Part A as settled.

The Spouse Path and the Medicaid Bar Are Not the Same Question

Premium-free Part A through a spouse solves the hospital-premium problem. It does not automatically solve the safety-net problem, and the difference has a legal basis families need to understand.

Under 8 U.S.C. § 1645, a spouse's qualifying quarters count toward the parent's own forty-quarter total during the marriage and during widowhood. In those situations, reaching forty quarters through the spouse generally lifts the five-year Medicaid bar at the same time it delivers Part A. The two arrive together, as long as the trapped quarters do not pull the qualifying count below forty, which is exactly what happened to Rosa Ramirez.

Divorce is the exception. A ten-year marriage can still provide premium-free Part A to a divorced parent. But once the marriage ends in divorce, the former spouse's quarters stop counting toward the parent's forty-quarter Medicaid exemption. So a divorced parent can hold premium-free Part A on the hospital side while still facing the five-year Medicaid bar on the safety-net side. The parent's own status and time as a permanent resident then decide the Medicaid picture.

State Medicaid rules vary, and the H.R.1 changes taking effect October 1, 2026, narrow eligibility for some immigrant categories. Verify the parent's Medicaid standing against current state and federal rules rather than assuming that Part A eligibility carries the safety net with it. Chapter 18 covers the means-tested side in full.

A Worked Count: The Okonkwo Marriage

Grace Okonkwo's mother, Ada, arrived at sixty-two with no U.S. work history. On her own, Ada will never reach forty credits before the buy-in decision matters. Grace assumed her mother faced the full $565 premium for life.

The spouse record changed that. Ada's husband, Daniel, worked in the United States for twenty-two years and holds well over forty credits, none of which overlapped a means-tested benefit. Daniel is sixty-six and already drawing Social Security. Grace checked the 2026 conditions for a currently married parent: the spouse has forty credits, the spouse is at least sixty-two, and the marriage has lasted at least one year. Ada and Daniel have been married for thirty-one years. All three conditions are met, so Ada qualifies for premium-free Part A on Daniel's record when she turns sixty-five. No buy-in premium at all.

Grace did not stop at Part A, because Part A and the safety net are separate questions. Ada and Daniel are married, so under 8 U.S.C. § 1645 Daniel's qualifying quarters count toward Ada's own forty-quarter total during the marriage. Because none of Daniel's quarters were trapped, his forty qualifying quarters carry over cleanly, and the spouse path delivers premium-free Part A and lifts the five-year Medicaid bar together. This is the outcome Rosa Ramirez could not reach, and the difference is only the two trapped quarters on the worker's record.

Grace noted the one scenario that would break this. If Ada and Daniel were to divorce, the ten-year marriage would still preserve Ada's premium-free Part A, but Daniel's quarters would stop counting toward Ada's Medicaid exemption, and Ada would face the five-year Medicaid bar on her own status. Because the marriage is intact, that risk is theoretical for now, and Grace logged it as a fact to revisit only if circumstances change.

She then called Social Security at 800-772-1213 to confirm Ada's specific eligibility before treating the plan as final.

What It Costs Without Forty Credits

When the credits are not there, and a spouse's record does not fill the gap, the parent buys into Part A. The 2026 costs are set.

A parent with 30 to 39 credits, or married to someone with at least 30 credits, pays the reduced Part A premium of $311 per month in 2026. A parent with fewer than 30 credits pays the full Part A premium of $565 per month in 2026.

At $565 per month, Part A alone costs $6,780 per year. Over a twenty-year retirement, that is a six-figure expense before any other Medicare cost. This is Leak Two from Chapter 3, and it is the reason the credit count matters so much.

Citizenship does not change these premiums. Naturalizing does not create work credits, and Part A cost stays tied to the credit record. What citizenship changes is the safety-net side and the permanence of status, as Chapter 5 explained. The premium math on this page is a credit question, not a citizenship question.

Action Checklist

- ☐ Pull the parent's Social Security earnings statement online at ssa.gov, or request a certified itemized statement using Form SSA-7050 if you need the year-by-year detail.

- ☐ Read the statement for two separate numbers: the quarters of coverage that decide premium-free Part A, and, only if the forty-quarter Medicaid route is needed, the qualifying quarters that decide the Medicaid exemption.
- ☐ To check for disqualified quarters, compare the earnings record against the family's own history of federal means-tested benefits, because Social Security does not show this. Any post-1996 quarter where taxed work overlapped SSI, TANF, non-emergency Medicaid, SNAP, or CHIP does not count toward the forty for the Medicaid exemption. It never affects the Part A count.
- ☐ If the parent is short on quarters of coverage for Part A, count the covered working years remaining before age sixty-five and decide whether finishing the count is realistic.
- ☐ If a spouse has forty credits, confirm the parent's marital situation against the 2026 conditions for current, divorced, and widowed spouses, and verify with Social Security at 800-772-1213.
- ☐ For a divorced parent, remember that premium-free Part A does not by itself lift the five-year Medicaid bar. Check the Medicaid picture separately against the parent's own status and permanent-resident time.
- ☐ If neither the parent's own credits nor a spouse's record reaches forty, price the buy-in at $311 or $565 per month for 2026 and fold that cost into the bridge-year plan in Chapters 11 and 12.
- ☐ Verify the parent's Medicaid standing against current state rules and the October 1, 2026 H.R.1 changes before assuming the safety net is in place. See Chapter 18.

CHAPTER 10

Disability: A Faster Door to Medicare

Marcus had run the timeline three times, and each time it ended the same way.

"My father is sixty-two," he told the counselor. "He had a stroke last year. He can't work, he has almost no credits, and he is three years short of sixty-five. What is he supposed to do until Medicare age?"

"There may be a faster door," the counselor said. "Disability. Your father is too young for Medicare by age, and that is the wall in front of him. But if he qualifies for disability, Medicare can open before he turns sixty-five. It runs on his work record and his medical condition, not on his age and not on how long he has lived here. Let's see whether that door is open to him."

For a parent under sixty-five, the ordinary door to Medicare is closed for one simple reason: they are not old enough yet. Neither a long work record nor five years of residence changes that, because both of those routes still wait for age sixty-five to arrive. Disability is the one path that ignores age entirely. This is what the chapter means by a faster door. It is not faster than the ordinary rules for someone who has already reached sixty-five. It is faster because it can reach Medicare years before sixty-five for a parent who cannot work and cannot wait. This chapter explains how that path works, what it requires, the coverage gap that comes with it, and the two conditions that move even faster.

The Fast Path: Disability to Medicare

A parent under sixty-five who cannot work because of a serious medical condition may qualify for Social Security Disability Insurance, known as SSDI. SSDI is not a need-based program, but an earned benefit, paid to workers who have enough credits and who meet the disability standard.

The reason SSDI matters here is what it leads to. A person who receives SSDI becomes eligible for Medicare after a twenty-four-month waiting period, measured from the date SSDI entitlement begins. A disabled parent who qualifies for SSDI can reach Medicare before age sixty-five, without satisfying the five-year residence rule, because Medicare through disability runs on the work record and the disability, not on residence. For a parent who is otherwise stuck behind the clock, this is often the only early door available.

Be clear about what SSDI is and is not doing, because it is easy to misread. SSDI is not a shortcut around the five-year residence rule for a parent who has already turned sixty-five. A parent at sixty-five or older who has forty lifetime credits is already exempt from the residence rule and does not need disability to enroll. And for a parent under sixty-five, waiving the residence rule buys nothing on its own, because age, not residence, is what stands in the way. This is why SSDI matters only for the under-sixty-five parent. It is the single route that reaches Medicare while a parent is still too young to qualify by age at all. Once a parent turns sixty-five, the ordinary doors open and SSDI is no longer the relevant path.

What SSDI Actually Requires

Two standards gate this path, and both are stricter than families expect.

The first is a work-credit standard, and it is not the same as the forty lifetime credits that make Part A free, even though the numbers look alike. This standard is called the 20/40 rule, and it has two parts that must both be met. The first part is a duration-of-work test. A worker aged thirty-one or older generally needs forty credits over their lifetime. The second part is a recent-work test, and this is the part with no equivalent anywhere else in Medicare. Of those credits, twenty must have been earned in the ten years ending when the disability began. Because a person can earn at most four credits a year, twenty credits equals about five years of work. In plain terms, the parent must have worked roughly five of the last ten years before the disability started.

The name itself confuses, so read it carefully. In "20/40," the forty refers to forty quarters of time, meaning the ten year window before the disability. It does not refer to the forty lifetime credits in the duration test, even though that number also appears. Two different forties are in play: forty quarters of look-back time, and forty lifetime credits of work.

The recent-work half is what most often closes this door for immigrant parents, and it closes it in a way families do not expect. A parent may have built a respectable lifetime credit count over past years of work and still fail, because those credits are old. Disability frequently arrives after a person has already stopped working, whether from an earlier decline in health, retirement, or caregiving at home. That is exactly when the recent-work window is most likely to be empty. So a rule that sounds like "you need forty credits" is really "you need to have been working recently," and that is a far harder bar for a parent who arrived late or left the workforce years before becoming disabled. One timing detail can matter here: the ten-year window is measured from the date the disability began, not from the date of application, so the relevant question is what the work record looked like at onset. Younger workers need fewer credits and a shorter recent-work history, but for a parent of typical retirement age the full 20/40 rule applies.

A short example makes the recent-work half concrete. Picture two parents, each aged sixty-two, each with a stroke in 2025, and each with exactly forty lifetime credits. The first, Mr. Abara, worked steadily from 2016 through 2024, then stopped when his health declined. Counting back ten years from his 2025 onset, he easily has twenty credits inside that window, because most of his work falls within it. He passes the 20/40 rule. The second, Mr. Costa, earned all forty of his credits between 2001 and 2011 and did no covered work after that. His lifetime total is identical, forty credits, but when SSA counts back ten years from 2025, the window reaches only to 2015, and Mr. Costa has zero credits inside it. He fails the recent-work test and cannot get SSDI, despite having the same forty credits as Mr. Abara. The difference is not how much they worked, but when.

The second is the disability standard itself, measured largely through substantial gainful activity, or SGA. To qualify, the parent must be unable to work above the SGA level. In 2026, that level is $1,690 per month for a non-blind person and $2,830 for a person who is blind. Earning above that at the time of application generally results in a finding that the parent is not disabled. The same SGA test continues after benefits begin, so a parent who later earns above the level can lose the benefit.

Both standards must be met. Enough recent credits alone will not qualify a parent who can still work above SGA, and a qualifying medical condition alone will not qualify a parent who lacks the recent credits.

The Coverage Gap During the Wait

The twenty-four-month waiting period is often misunderstood, so be precise about what it is and is not. There are actually two separate delays to plan around. First, for most claimants, the SSDI cash benefit does not begin until after a five-month waiting period, with the first payment made in the sixth full month after the date the disability is found to have begun. Second, once the cash benefit begins, the parent still has no Medicare coverage until the twenty-four-month Medicare waiting period ends. During those twenty-four months, the parent does receive the SSDI cash benefit. Money comes in. What does not come in is Medicare.

So the wait is not a cash cost, but a coverage gap. The parent needs some way to stay medically covered for up to two years between the start of SSDI and the start of Medicare. For a low-income parent, that bridge is often Medicaid or a marketplace plan, and the choices are the subject of Chapter 11. The point to hold here is that qualifying for SSDI solves the eventual Medicare question but leaves a two-year hole that has to be planned for, not a bill that has to be paid.

It helps to see SSDI as delivering two different things on two different clocks. It does not make the road to Medicare short, because the twenty-four-month wait is fixed and cannot be shortened. What it does provide during that road is income. Once the five-month cash waiting period passes, the SSDI check arrives every month, including through the entire twenty-four-month Medicare gap. So a family should plan for SSDI to cover part of the parent's living costs during the wait, while arranging separate medical coverage to fill the Medicare gap itself.

One more point decides whether this path is worth taking. Because Medicare through disability arrives twenty-four months after entitlement, SSDI only reaches Medicare earlier than age sixty-five would when the parent is far enough below sixty-five for that twenty-four-month clock to still land before their sixty-fifth birthday. For a parent at sixty-two, the disability path can open Medicare around age sixty-four, well ahead of the ordinary door. For a parent already past sixty-three, the twenty-four-month wait may finish at or after sixty-five, at which point simply reaching Medicare age is the faster route and SSDI adds nothing to the timing. Weigh the parent's current age against the twenty-four months before treating disability as the fast path, because for a parent close to sixty-five it may not be fast at all.

The Faster Path: ALS and ESRD

Two conditions bypass the twenty-four-month wait entirely, and families facing them should know this immediately.

A person diagnosed with ALS, amyotrophic lateral sclerosis, qualifies for Medicare the month their SSDI benefits begin, with no waiting period. A person with end-stage renal disease, meaning kidney failure requiring dialysis or a transplant, can qualify for Medicare under a separate set of timing rules that also move faster than the standard path.

These are narrow doors, but for the families they apply to, they are the fastest route to coverage available. If a parent has either diagnosis, raise it with Social Security at once, because the timing rules are different from everything else in this chapter.

A Worked Timeline: Marcus's Father

Marcus's father, Elias, is sixty-two. He became a permanent resident in October 2022, sponsored by Marcus. Elias worked in the United States for parts of eight years before his stroke in early 2025, and his earnings record shows enough recent credits to be insured for SSDI. He is not a citizen, and he is far from forty lifetime quarters.

In early 2025, Elias's stroke leaves him unable to work above the SGA level, and he applies for SSDI in March 2025. Because he has the recent work credits and a qualifying condition, he is approved. After the five-month cash waiting period, his SSDI cash benefit begins in 2025, and that entitlement date is what starts his twenty-four-month Medicare clock.

From 2025 through 2027 comes the coverage gap. Elias receives the SSDI cash benefit once the five-month wait passes, but he has no Medicare during the twenty-four-month wait that follows. Because he is only sixty-two, he cannot reach Medicare by age either, so disability is his only early door. The family bridges the medical gap with a Chapter 11 option and leans on the SSDI cash to help with living costs in the meantime.

In 2027, twenty-four months after his SSDI entitlement, Elias becomes eligible for Medicare through disability, at age sixty-four, roughly a year before he would reach Medicare age on his own. The fast path worked, and it worked precisely because he was young enough for the twenty-four month wait to still land before sixty-five. The need-based help he would still like, SSI and a Medicare Savings Program, remains complicated by the deeming from Marcus's sponsorship. For a disabled, sponsored parent, this means citizenship or the forty-quarter mark is the event that unlocks the need-based help around Medicare, so plan the disability path and that milestone together. Elias reached Medicare early through disability. The help around it waits on naturalization.

Action Checklist

- ☐ If a parent under sixty-five cannot work because of a serious medical condition, ask Social Security whether they are insured for SSDI, which generally requires forty credits with twenty earned in the last ten years for a worker aged thirty-one or older.
- ☐ Remember this path only helps a parent under sixty-five. Its purpose is to reach Medicare before Medicare age. A parent already sixty-five with forty lifetime credits does not need disability, and a parent close to sixty-five may reach age sixty-five sooner than the twenty-four-month wait would deliver Medicare.
- ☐ Check the recent-work half of the 20/40 rule, not just the lifetime total. A parent with old credits but no recent work can fail, because twenty credits must fall in the ten years before the disability began.
- ☐ Remember the SSDI disability standard uses substantial gainful activity: in 2026, $1,690 per month for a non-blind person and $2,830 for a person who is blind, tested both at application and after benefits begin.
- ☐ Understand that SSDI leads to Medicare after a twenty-four-month waiting period, which opens Medicare before age sixty-five and without the five-year residence rule.
- ☐ Plan for two delays: a five-month wait before the SSDI cash benefit begins, and the twenty-four-month coverage gap before Medicare begins. The parent receives cash during the Medicare gap but has no Medicare, so arrange bridge coverage through Chapter 11.
- ☐ Raise any ALS or ESRD diagnosis with Social Security immediately, since both bypass the standard twenty-four-month wait.
- ☐ Remember that disability opens Medicare but not the need-based help around it. The SSDI cash benefit and Medicare are safe from deeming, but for a sponsored parent, deeming can still block SSI and the Medicare Savings Programs. See Chapter 7.
- ☐ Plan the need-based side around the deeming exit that is realistic, usually citizenship, and build the full sequence with Chapter 12.

- [ ] Verify current disability rules with a benefits counselor before acting, since the SGA levels and credit rules change.

CHAPTER 11

Bridge Coverage: How to Stay Covered Affordably

"So He Just Has Nothing Until Then?"

Nadia had finally mapped her father's path to Medicare, but the map had a hole in the middle.

"He's sixty-three," she told the counselor. "His green card is three years old, so the residence rule doesn't let him buy into Medicare for two more years. He has no work credits. What does he do for health coverage in the meantime?"

"That gap is the hardest part of this whole process," the counselor said. "The rules that decide his Medicare and Medicaid don't leave him with nothing, but the good options are fewer than they used to be. We have to go through them one by one and see which ones he can actually reach."

The bridge years are the stretch between the day a parent needs coverage and the day Medicare or Medicaid finally opens. Chapter 10 showed one common source of that gap, the twenty-four months between SSDI and Medicare. The residence rule creates another. This chapter walks through the coverage options that can carry a parent across, in order of who they fit, and it is honest about a real change that has narrowed the best of them. It also introduces a set of limited products that can provide a bare floor of protection when nothing better is available, and explains why a good agent matters more here than almost anywhere else in this book.

Start With Coverage the Parent Already Has Access To

The first question is whether the parent can reach coverage through work, their own, or a family member's.

A parent still working may have an employer plan, and a parent whose spouse works may be able to join the spouse's plan. An adult child's employer plan generally cannot cover a parent, since parents are rarely eligible dependents, so this route usually runs through the parent's or the spouse's own job. Where it exists, employer coverage is often the most complete option available during the bridge, because it is comprehensive insurance with full protections. Check this first, before anything else, because it can make the rest of the chapter unnecessary.

COBRA: A Time-Limited Bridge

A parent who is leaving a job that provided health coverage can usually keep that same plan for a limited time through COBRA (Consolidated Omnibus Budget Reconciliation Act). COBRA lets a former employee continue the employer group plans for up to eighteen months in most cases.

The catch is cost. Under COBRA, the parent pays the full premium, both the share they used to pay and the share the employer previously covered, plus a small administrative fee. That can be expensive. But COBRA has real strengths for a bridge. It is the same comprehensive coverage the parent already had, it accepts pre-existing conditions without limitation, and its eighteen-month clock can line up well with a bridge that has a known end date, such as the wait for Medicare. For a parent leaving work within about a year and a half of Medicare eligibility, COBRA can be the cleanest bridge available, if the family can absorb the premium.

The ACA Marketplace: Narrower Than It Used to Be

For years, the Affordable Care Act marketplace was the standard bridge for a low-income immigrant parent. A lawfully present parent could buy a marketplace plan, and premium tax credits often brought the cost within reach even for those inside the five-year Medicaid bar. That picture has changed, and a family planning today needs the current version, not the old one.

Lawful permanent residents can still buy marketplace coverage, and those whose income qualifies can still receive premium tax credits to lower the cost. For many middle-income LPR parents, the marketplace remains a workable bridge.

The change hits the lowest-income parents hardest, and it is the group this book most often describes. Beginning in January 2026, lawfully present immigrants with income below the federal poverty level who do not qualify for Medicaid because of their immigration status can no longer receive premium tax credits for a marketplace plan. This is exactly the position of a poor parent inside the five-year Medicaid bar. For years, that parent leaned on subsidized marketplace coverage. As of 2026, that subsidy is gone for the below-poverty group, which can leave the marketplace plan unaffordable at full price. A further narrowing takes effect in January 2027, when the definition of who qualifies for marketplace financial help tightens again, though lawful permanent residents whose income qualifies remain eligible.

The practical lesson is to check marketplace eligibility carefully and against current rules, because the answer now depends heavily on the parent's income and exact status. A middle-income LPR may find the marketplace works well. A below-poverty LPR inside the Medicaid bar may find the subsidized door has closed, and that is the parent for whom the rest of this chapter matters most.

Medicaid, Where the Parent Can Reach It

If the parent is past the five-year bar, or falls into a category exempt from it, full Medicaid may be available and is usually the strongest bridge of all, because it is comprehensive and low-cost or free. Chapter 6 explained when the bar lifts, and Chapter 18 covers Medicaid in full.

Two points belong here. First, emergency Medicaid is available to an otherwise-eligible parent regardless of the five-year bar, so a parent in the gap is never entirely without a backstop for a true emergency, though it covers only emergency care. Second, the October 1, 2026 H.R.1 changes narrow which immigrant categories qualify for Medicaid, so confirm the parent's current standing rather than assuming eligibility. For a parent who can reach it, Medicaid ends the bridge problem. For a parent still inside the bar, it is not yet an option, and the limited tools below may be all that remain.

When the Good Options Are Closed: A Floor, Not a Solution

Some parents will reach this point in the chapter without a workable option above. No employer plan, no affordable COBRA, no marketplace subsidy, and still inside the Medicaid bar. This is the hardest case, and it is more common now than it was before 2026. For these families, a set of limited products can provide a partial floor of protection. None of them is comprehensive coverage, and none is a substitute for the Medicare foundation the parent is working toward. They are what stands between the parent and having nothing.

This is the protection layer of the three layers of dignity, appearing early and in a stripped-down form. In the bridge years, its job is narrow: a bare minimum that reduces exposure while the parent crosses to Medicare. In Chapter 15, once the Medicare foundation is in place, this same layer takes on a fuller and more active role. Here, keep the purpose modest.

Supplemental Fixed-Benefit Plans

Supplemental fixed-benefit plans are a form of limited insurance. They include hospital indemnity plans, critical illness plans, cancer plans, and dementia coverage. Unlike comprehensive insurance, they do not cover the broad range of a person's medical care. Instead, each pays a fixed cash amount when a specific covered event happens. A hospital indemnity plan pays a set amount per day or per hospital stay. A critical illness or cancer plan pays a lump sum on the diagnosis of a covered condition. Dementia coverage pays on a qualifying diagnosis.

Their value in the bridge years is that they are usually affordable and can cushion the financial blow of a major event, such as a hospitalization or a serious diagnosis, that would otherwise fall entirely on the family. Their limits are just as important to understand. Benefits are capped and tied to specific events, so they will not pay for routine or unexpected care outside those triggers. Many reduce or exclude benefits for pre-existing conditions, which matters greatly for an older parent who likely has some. They are a safety net, and a family should treat them as reducing risk on specific events rather than providing real coverage.

Health Care Sharing Programs

Families researching bridge options will encounter health care sharing programs, sometimes called health shares. It is worth knowing plainly what they are and how widely they are used, because they are a real and established option that many people choose.

A health care sharing program is not the same as insurance. It is typically a membership organization, often faith-based, in which members pay a monthly amount that is used to share one another's eligible medical costs. It can resemble insurance from the outside, and its monthly cost is often lower than a full-price health plan. These programs are neither fringe nor rare. About 1.5 million Americans participate in them, the federal government has certified more than one hundred sharing ministries, members are found in every state, and the programs collectively share over a billion dollars in medical costs each year. Membership grew sharply after the Affordable Care Act, roughly ninefold over about seven years, which tells you that a large number of families have found them a workable answer to the cost of coverage. For a healthy member facing a high full-price premium, a health share can meaningfully lower monthly cost, and many members report satisfaction with them.

Two features distinguish a health share from insurance, and a family should weigh them before deciding. First, because these programs are not insurance, the sharing of any given medical cost is generally structured as voluntary rather than as a contractual promise to pay, and most programs say so plainly in their own guidelines. Members submit eligible costs for sharing, and the programs do share a large volume of expenses, but a family should read the program's terms to understand how sharing decisions are made and what options exist if a cost is not shared. Second, health shares commonly limit or exclude pre-existing conditions, and they may exclude some other categories of care. For an older parent who likely has existing health conditions, that limitation can leave the most probable expenses unshared.

The balance, then, is real on both sides. A health share is an affordable, widely used option that works well for some members, and it carries a payment structure and pre-existing-condition rules that make it a poorer fit for others, particularly seniors with existing conditions. It is presented here so families know the option exists and understand how it works. Whether it fits is the family's decision.

Why an Agent Matters Most Here

Nowhere in the bridge-year decision does professional help pay off more than in this thin, complicated space. The options are uneven, the rules changed recently, and the limited products vary widely in quality, with some sound and some predatory. A parent or family navigating this alone can easily buy the wrong thing.

A knowledgeable Medicare or health insurance agent does three things that are hard to do alone. First, they match a limited product to the parent's actual health and budget, so a family does not pay for a plan whose exclusions make it useless for that parent's conditions. Second, they screen out unsuitable and predatory offerings, which are common in exactly the corner of the market a desperate family is pushed toward when the good options close. Third, they coordinate the bridge as a whole, lining up whatever partial protections are available with the date Medicare or Medicaid will finally open, so the pieces fit the timeline. Ask the agent directly what a product does not cover, how pre-existing conditions are treated, and whether it is insurance at all. A good agent will answer plainly. Chapter 19 covers how to build your Medicare team, and this bridge decision is one of the best reasons to have one.

What to Bring to the Agent for the Bridge Decision

Tell the agent the parent's exact status and income, because those decide whether the marketplace subsidy is still available. Tell them the parent's known health conditions, because pre-existing-condition limits are the single biggest reason a limited product fails a senior. Tell them the target date the bridge needs to reach, usually the Medicare or Medicaid opening, so the coverage can be timed to it. Then ask three questions about any product offered: Is this insurance? What does it not cover? How are pre-existing conditions handled? The agent's job here is to match, screen, and coordinate, not to sell you the first plan on the shelf. If an offer is rushed or the answers are vague, treat that as a warning.

Action Checklist

- ☐ Check first for employer or spousal coverage, because where it exists it is usually the most complete bridge available.
- ☐ If the parent is leaving a job with coverage, price COBRA. It is expensive but comprehensive, accepts pre-existing conditions, and lasts up to eighteen months, which can match a known bridge.
- ☐ Check ACA marketplace eligibility against current rules. A middle-income LPR may still get premium tax credits, but a below-poverty LPR inside the Medicaid bar generally lost that subsidy as of January 2026.

- ☐ Confirm whether the parent is past the five-year Medicaid bar or exempt, because Medicaid, where reachable, is the strongest bridge. Remember emergency Medicaid is always available for a true emergency.
- ☐ If no comprehensive option is reachable, understand the limited tools as a floor only: supplemental fixed-benefit plans pay fixed amounts on specific events and often limit pre-existing conditions.
- ☐ Know that a health care sharing program is a widely used, lower-cost option but is not insurance: it carries no legal guarantee of payment and typically limits pre-existing conditions, which matters most for an older parent. Weigh both sides before deciding.
- ☐ Involve a Medicare or health insurance agent to match products to the parent's health and budget, screen out predatory offerings, and coordinate the bridge to the Medicare or Medicaid start date. See Chapter 19.
- ☐ Verify every eligibility rule against current law, because immigrant bridge-coverage rules changed in 2026 and 2027 and remain in active flux.

CHAPTER 12

Building the Bridge Plan for Your Profile

"Just Tell Me What to Do"

By her third meeting, Priya had read enough to feel more lost, not less.

"I understand the rules now," she told the counselor. "The two clocks, the credits, the deeming, the coverage options. But I have all these pieces and no plan. Just tell me what my mother should actually do, in order."

"That's the right question," the counselor said. "The pieces are the same for everyone. The order in which you use them depends on which parent you have. Let's build your mother's plan, step by step, for her profile."

This chapter turns everything from Chapters 6 through 10 into a plan. Chapter 8 told you which of four profiles your parent fits. This chapter takes each profile and lays out the moves in sequence: what to secure first, how to bridge the gap, and what event finally ends the bridge. Read the section for your parent's profile closely, and skim the others, because parents sometimes shift from one profile to another as facts are confirmed.

The Four Questions Every Plan Answers

Every bridge plan, whatever the profile, answers the same four questions in order. Keep them in mind as you read your profile's section.

First, what does the parent need coverage for, and starting when? Second, what is the endpoint, meaning the event that finally opens Medicare or Medicaid and ends the bridge? Third, what carries the parent across the gap in between? Fourth, what single move most shortens or removes the bridge altogether? For most profiles, that last move is citizenship or reaching forty quarters, but not for all.

Profile A: The Worker

The Worker has forty credits of their own, so most of the hard problems are already solved. Part A is free, the Medicare residence rule does not apply, deeming has ended, and the five-year Medicaid bar is lifted. There is usually no long bridge to build.

The plan here is short. Confirm the forty credits on the Social Security earnings record, so the free Part A is certain rather than assumed. Enroll in Medicare on time, during the correct window, because the Worker's main risk is not eligibility but a late-enrollment penalty, which Chapters 13 and 14 cover. Treat citizenship as worthwhile for permanence and to remove public-charge exposure, but not urgent for coverage. For the Worker, the bridge is short or nonexistent, and the work shifts to choosing coverage well, which is Part 5.

Profile B: The Late Arrival

The Late Arrival is the hardest case and needs the most deliberate plan. This parent arrived near or after age sixty, has few or no credits, faces the full Medicare residence rule and the five-year welfare bar, and cannot realistically reach forty quarters.

Answer the four questions in order. The coverage need usually begins at age sixty-five, when the parent wants Medicare but cannot yet buy in through residence. The endpoint is the later of two dates: when five continuous years of residence are complete, opening the Medicare buy-in, and when the five-year welfare bar lifts, opening full Medicaid. Chart both dates from Chapter 6. The bridge across the gap comes from Chapter 10, and here the plan must be honest about the 2026 change: a below-poverty Late Arrival inside the Medicaid bar likely lost the marketplace subsidy, so the realistic bridge may be a spouse's or employer plan if one exists, emergency Medicaid for true emergencies, and, where nothing else reaches, the limited protection-floor tools, all coordinated with an agent.

Because the Late Arrival often lacks forty credits, this parent may face a Part A premium rather than premium-free Part A. When that happens, the rule is to enroll in Part B and Part D on time regardless of the Part A decision, because those penalties run independently, and then rely on full Medicaid or a Medicare Savings Program to pay the Part A and Part B premiums and erase the penalties for a parent who qualifies. Chapter 18 explains how this works and how to apply.

The single most powerful move for the Late Arrival is citizenship. Naturalization removes the residence rule, lifts the welfare bar, satisfies the SSI wait, and ends any deeming, all at once. It is the one move that can collapse the entire bridge. Bear in mind, though, that citizenship is not immediate: naturalizing generally requires five years as a permanent resident and meeting the other requirements, including an English and a civics test, so the citizenship track takes time to mature and must be started early. Senior exemptions and the full process are in Chapter 5 and Chapter 22. So the Late Arrival's plan runs on two tracks at the same time: bridge coverage for the immediate gap, and a citizenship timeline aimed at ending the bridge as early as eligibility allows.

Profile C: The Sponsored Parent

The Sponsored Parent carries everything the Late Arrival does, plus deeming from a sponsor's Affidavit of Support. The plan is the Late Arrival's plan with one addition: deeming has to be planned around, because it can block the need-based help the parent would otherwise lean on during the bridge.

Work the four questions as for the Late Arrival, then add the deeming layer from Chapter 7. During the bridge, assume that SSI, and in some states Medicaid, may be blocked by the sponsor's deemed income, so do not build the plan around need-based help the parent cannot actually get. Where a denial happens, ask about the indigence exception before accepting it. Note also that a sponsor can be asked to repay certain benefits the parent does receive, which is a reason to understand deeming before applying for anything.

Like the Late Arrival, the Sponsored Parent often lacks forty credits and may owe a Part A premium. The same rule applies: enroll in Part B and Part D on time regardless of the Part A decision, and, once deeming allows the parent to qualify, use full Medicaid or a Medicare Savings Program to pay the premiums and erase the penalties. Because deeming can delay that qualification, this is one more reason to plan the deeming exit and the premium help together, as Chapter 18 describes.

The exits from deeming are the same events that help elsewhere: forty quarters, which a late-arriving parent usually cannot reach, or citizenship, which usually can be reached, though only after the five-year permanent-resident wait and the naturalization requirements are met. So for the

Sponsored Parent, as for the Late Arrival, citizenship is the move that does the most, because it ends deeming and lifts the eligibility bars together. The bridge plan holds the parent steady while the citizenship timeline runs.

Profile D: The Spouse-Credit Parent

The Spouse-Credit Parent has the most hopeful plan of the harder profiles, because a spouse's record can deliver premium-free Part A without the parent ever earning forty credits alone. This can move a parent who looked like a Late Arrival close to the Worker's position.

The first move is to confirm the spouse's record against the 2026 conditions from Chapter 9: a current spouse with forty credits who is at least sixty-two and married to the parent at least a year, a former spouse from a marriage that lasted at least ten years with the parent now single, or a deceased spouse, meaning the parent is widowed, from a marriage that lasted at least nine months with the parent now single. Verify this with Social Security before building on it, because it changes the whole plan. If it holds, Part A is free, and the Medicare residence rule falls away, since the parent then qualifies through the work record.

The plan must still handle the Medicaid side separately, and this is where the caution from Chapter 9 lives. When the qualifying quarters come through a current or widowed spouse, the five-year Medicaid bar generally lifts along with Part A, so the bridge on the need-based side is short. When they come through a divorced spouse, premium-free Part A survives but the former spouse's quarters stop counting toward the Medicaid exemption, so the parent may still face the five-year bar and needs a bridge for the need-based side. Confirm which case applies, then bridge only the gap that remains.

When a Parent Shifts Profiles Mid-Plan

Profiles are not always fixed, and a plan should be ready to change when a fact is confirmed. A parent who looked like a Late Arrival may turn out to be a Spouse-Credit Parent once a spouse's record is examined, which shortens the bridge dramatically. A Sponsored Parent approaches the Late Arrival's plan as the deeming exit nears. A parent building credits may cross from Late Arrival toward Worker if forty quarters come into reach.

The rule from Chapter 8 still governs. Plan for the more demanding profile first, then adjust downward as better facts are confirmed. It is safer to prepare a longer bridge and be pleasantly surprised than to assume a short one and be caught without coverage. Revisit the plan whenever a new fact arrives, especially a confirmed spouse's record, a credit total, or a citizenship eligibility date.

What the Agent Needs to Build the Plan with You

Give the agent the parent's profile first, because it sets the entire sequence. For the Worker, the agent's focus is timely enrollment and plan choice. For the Late Arrival and Sponsored Parent, the agent needs the two five-year dates and the sponsorship fact, so bridge coverage can be timed to the end point, and need-based help is not assumed where deeming blocks it. For the Spouse-Credit Parent, the agent needs the spouse's record details and whether the marriage is current, divorced, or widowed, because that decides whether the Medicaid bar lifts with Part A. In every profile, the agent coordinates the bridge coverage to the date the bridge ends. Bring the profile and the key dates, and the agent can assemble the pieces into a timed plan.

Action Checklist

- ☐ Identify your parent's profile from Chapter 8 before building anything, because it sets the order of every move.
- ☐ Answer the four questions in sequence: what coverage is needed and when, what event ends the bridge, what carries the parent across, and what single move most shortens the bridge.
- ☐ For the Worker, confirm the forty credits, enroll on time to avoid penalties, and treat citizenship as useful but not urgent.
- ☐ For the Late Arrival, chart both five-year dates, build honest bridge coverage under the 2026 rules, and run a citizenship timeline as the move that collapses the bridge.
- ☐ For the Sponsored Parent, add the deeming layer: do not assume need-based help during the bridge, ask about the indigence exception on any denial, and aim citizenship at ending deeming.
- ☐ For a parent without premium-free Part A, usually the Late Arrival or Sponsored Parent, enroll in Part B and Part D on time and use full Medicaid or a Medicare Savings Program to pay the premiums and erase the penalties. See Chapter 18.
- ☐ For the Spouse-Credit Parent, verify the spouse's record with Social Security, then bridge only the Medicaid gap that remains, which depends on whether the spouse is current, divorced, or widowed.
- ☐ Revisit the plan whenever a new fact arrives, and adjust the profile if a spouse's record, a credit total, or a citizenship date changes the picture.
- ☐ Involve an agent to time the bridge coverage to the endpoint, and bring the profile and key dates so the plan fits the parent's real situation.

CHAPTER 13

Enrollment Windows and the Employer Escape Hatch

Daniel thought he had done everything right. His mother turned sixty-five in the spring; she had her green card, she had lived in the country long enough, and he assumed Medicare would simply begin the way a birthday arrives, on its own, without anyone having to act. He was busy that spring. Work was heavy, his mother felt well, and there was no letter that forced the question. The months passed the way months do when nothing seems wrong.

Then his mother needed care, and Daniel learned three things in the same afternoon: Nothing had started, a window had opened and closed while he waited, and the cost of the delay would not be a one-time fee that he could pay and forget. It would be added to her premium every month for the rest of her life. None of it had to happen. A single date on a calendar would have prevented all of it.

This chapter is about those dates. Medicare enrollment is not automatic for most immigrant parents, and the penalty for missing the window is one of the few Medicare costs that is both permanent and entirely avoidable. Enrollment feels like it should take care of itself, the way turning sixty-five takes care of itself, and that assumption is exactly what costs families the most. The whole of this chapter reduces to one instruction repeated in three parts: know the deadline, know whether current employment coverage protects the parent, and enroll within the correct window.

The Initial Enrollment Period

The first window is called the Initial Enrollment Period. It lasts seven months. It begins three months before the month the parent turns sixty-five, it includes the birthday month, and it runs three months after. For a parent turning sixty-five in May, the window opens in February and closes at the end of August.

When coverage actually begins depends on when the parent signs up inside that window. Coverage always starts on the first of a month. If the parent enrolls in the three months before the birthday month, coverage begins the first day of the birthday month, with no gap. If the parent enrolls during the birthday month or in the three months after, coverage is pushed to the first day of the following month or later. The lesson is simple. Enroll in the three months before turning sixty-five, so coverage is in force on the first possible day.

One detail changes the timing. A parent born on the first of the month is treated, for Medicare purposes, as turning sixty-five in the previous month, so the entire Initial Enrollment Period shifts one month earlier. An example makes this clear. A parent born on June 1 is treated as turning sixty-five in May, not June. Her seven-month window therefore opens in February, three months before May, and closes at the end of August. A parent born on June 2, only one day later, is treated as turning sixty-five in June, so her window opens in March and closes at the end of September. The single day of birth moves every date in the window by a full month. A family should check the birthday against this rule before counting the window.

Not Every Parent Should Rush to Enroll at Sixty-Five

The instruction to enroll on time has one important exception. A parent who has creditable coverage from a current job, their own or a spouse's, can safely delay Part B without a penalty. For that parent, enrolling at sixty-five may mean paying a premium for coverage they do not yet need. The key takeaway is to enroll on time unless current employment coverage protects the delay.

Everything so far assumes the parent is allowed to enroll at sixty-five in the first place. For two kinds of immigrant parents, that assumption does not hold, and it helps to separate two questions that are easy to blur together. The first question is whether the parent can enroll in Medicare at all. The second question is, once enrolled, whether Part A comes free or has to be paid for. These are different doors, controlled by different rules.

Consider the Late Arrival, a parent who came to the United States later in life. This parent may be blocked at the first door. Medicare has a residence rule, explained in Chapter 6, that requires a lawful permanent resident to have lived in the country for five continuous years before enrolling. A parent who reached sixty-five but has been here only two or three years simply cannot enroll yet. The birthday has arrived, but the door has not opened. She must wait until the five years are complete, and only then does her enrollment window apply.

Now consider the Sponsored Parent, a parent brought over by a family sponsor who has met the residence rule. This parent is past the first door. She can enroll, and here the warning of this whole chapter applies with full weight. Once a parent is eligible and has no current-employment coverage protecting a delay, the enrollment window is not optional. She must enroll in Part A and Part B during that window or the penalty clock begins.

This is where the Part A premium becomes a trap. A Sponsored Parent who lacks the forty-credit work record sees that Part A will cost a monthly premium, and the natural reaction is to hesitate, to skip enrollment, to wait until the money feels easier. That hesitation is the mistake. Skipping the window to avoid the Part A premium does not pause anything. It starts two penalties at once. The parent will owe a late penalty on the bought-in Part A, and a separate late penalty on Part B, and the Part B penalty is permanent. The very premium she was trying to avoid comes back larger, and Part B is added on top of it.

The right move is the opposite of the instinct. A Sponsored Parent who must buy into Part A should still enroll on time, pay the premium, and avoid turning a manageable monthly cost into two lifelong penalties. Premium-free Part A depends on a work record of forty credits, as Chapter 9 explained, and a parent who never built that record does not lose the right to enroll and does not escape the duty to enroll on time. She simply pays a premium for Part A instead of receiving it free.

Keeping these two doors separate prevents a common and costly mistake. A missing work record never blocks enrollment. It only decides whether Part A is free or purchased. Residence decides whether the parent can walk through the door at all. Confusing the two leads families either to give up on enrollment they are entitled to, or to assume enrollment is free when a Part A premium is actually due.

The Employer Escape Hatch

The most valuable exception to the sixty-five deadline is current employment coverage. As long as the parent, or the parent's spouse, is actively working and covered by that job's health plan, the Part B penalty clock does not run. The parent can wait, without penalty, for as long as the current-job coverage lasts.

When that coverage ends, a window opens. It is one of Medicare's Special Enrollment Periods, and it lasts eight months from the month the job or the job-based coverage ends, whichever comes first. Enrolling inside those eight months carries no penalty. Missing them sends the parent to the General Enrollment Period and starts the penalty running.

The Four Traps Inside the Escape Hatch

The employer escape hatch works only when the coverage truly counts as current-employment coverage. Four common situations look like protection but are not. Each one leaves the penalty clock running even though the parent believes they are covered.

Coverage type	Does it stop the Part B penalty?	Why
COBRA	No	COBRA is continuation coverage, not current-employment coverage. It does not pause the penalty clock, and it does not open a Special Enrollment Period when it ends.
Retiree coverage	No	Retiree plans come from past employment, not current work. They do not count as current-employment coverage for delaying Part B.
Employer with fewer than 20 employees	No	At a small employer, Medicare becomes the primary payer at sixty-five. The parent must enroll in Part B on time, because the small-group plan pays only after Medicare.
ACA marketplace plan	No	A marketplace plan is not employer coverage. It is not creditable for delaying Part B, and it does not open a Special Enrollment Period.

The rule beneath all four is the same. Only coverage from a current job, the parent's own or a spouse's, at an employer large enough to remain the primary payer, protects the parent from the Part B penalty. Anything else leaves the clock running.

The Escape Hatch Done Right: Mr. Osei

Mr. Osei turned sixty-five in March, and unlike Daniel's mother, he was still working. He held a full-time job at a company with more than two hundred employees, and he was covered by that company's health plan. His daughter Ama wanted to know whether he had to enroll in Part B in March to avoid a penalty.

He did not. Because Mr. Osei had coverage from a current job at a large employer, the escape hatch applied. His Initial Enrollment Period came and went in the spring, and he let it pass on purpose. The Part B penalty clock did not run because current employment coverage protected the delay. He kept working, kept his employer plan, and paid no Part B premium for coverage he did not yet need.

Two years later, at sixty-seven, Mr. Osei retired. His last day of work was June 30, and his employer coverage ended that same month. This is the moment that decides everything, and it is where families most often stumble. From the month the job or the job-based coverage ends, an eight-month Special Enrollment Period opens. For Mr. Osei, that window ran from July through the following February. Enrolling anywhere inside those eight months carried no penalty.

Ama did not wait. She helped her father enroll in Part B in July, the first full month after his coverage ended, and asked for coverage to begin August 1 so there would be no gap. He moved from the employer plan straight onto Medicare with no penalty and no uncovered stretch. Had he instead assumed that retiree coverage or a COBRA offer would hold the line, the clock would have kept running, and by the time he finally enrolled he would have carried a lifelong penalty for the delay.

The contrast with Daniel's mother is the whole lesson of this chapter. Both parents let the Initial Enrollment Period pass. One was protected because he had current employment coverage and acted inside the eight-month window when it ended. The other was not protected, because a birthday is not a form, and no coverage was standing in the gap. The difference between them was not luck. It was knowing which window applied and enrolling inside it.

How to Actually Enroll

Knowing the window is not the same as walking through the door. A family still has to file the enrollment, and how they do it depends on the parent's situation.

First, check whether enrollment is automatic. A parent who is already receiving Social Security benefits at least four months before turning sixty-five is enrolled in Part A and Part B automatically, with no application needed. Most immigrant parents in this book are not drawing Social Security that early, so for them nothing is automatic. They must apply.

For a parent signing up for the first time, the simplest route is online at the Social Security website, which handles Part A and Part B together in one application. A family can also apply by calling Social Security or by visiting a local office. If the parent already has Part A and is adding Part B later, for example after leaving a job, the form is the CMS-40B, the Application for Enrollment in Medicare Part B, submitted to the local Social Security office by mail or fax, or by the Social Security website. When a

Special Enrollment Period applies because a job is ending, the employer completes a separate form, the CMS-L564, confirming the dates of the coverage, and it is submitted with the application.

One practical habit prevents most problems. When filing, state plainly the month coverage should begin, and keep a dated copy of everything submitted. Enrollment disputes are far easier to resolve when the family can show exactly what was filed and when.

The General Enrollment Period

If a parent misses both the Initial Enrollment Period and any Special Enrollment Period, one path remains. The General Enrollment Period runs January 1 through March 31 each year. A parent who enrolls then will usually face a late enrollment penalty, unless they qualify for a Special Enrollment Period. How that penalty is calculated, how large it becomes, and whether it can ever be undone are the subject of the next chapter.

Action Checklist

- ☐ Mark the parent's Initial Enrollment Period on a calendar: the three months before the birthday month, the birthday month, and the three months after. Note that a first-of-the-month birthday shifts the window one month earlier.
- ☐ Enroll in the three months before the birthday month whenever possible, so coverage is effective the first day of eligibility with no gap.
- ☐ Check whether the parent is already receiving Social Security four months before sixty-five, which triggers automatic enrollment. If not, plan to apply actively.

- ☐ Determine whether the parent has current-employment coverage from their own or a spouse's active job, since only that coverage safely delays Part B.
- ☐ For a Sponsored Parent who must buy in to Part A, enroll on time anyway. Skipping the window to avoid the Part A premium starts penalties on both Part A and Part B.
- ☐ Check the four traps against the parent's situation: COBRA, retiree coverage, an employer with fewer than 20 employees, and any ACA marketplace plan. None of these protect against the Part B penalty.
- ☐ If current-employment coverage applies, confirm the employer has 20 or more employees, or the parent must still enroll in Part B on time.
- ☐ When that coverage ends, use the eight-month Special Enrollment Period to enroll without penalty, and do not wait for the General Enrollment Period. Have the employer complete form CMS-L564 to document the coverage dates.
- ☐ Keep a dated copy of every form submitted, and state the intended coverage start month in writing.
- ☐ If the parent missed every window, expect the General Enrollment Period of January 1 through March 31, and see Chapter 14 for how penalties are calculated and whether they can be undone.
- ☐ Verify every enrollment rule against current law, because immigrant Medicare timing rules continue to change.

CHAPTER 14

The Three Penalties and How to Undo Them

"It says my premium is two hundred and forty dollars," Mr. Serrano said, holding the letter at arm's length. "But you told me it would be one hundred and eighty."

Renata took the letter and read it twice. "There's a line here. Late enrollment penalty. They added it because you signed up two years after you turned sixty-five."

"Two years." Her father set down his coffee. "But I was fine then. I did not need the doctor. Why should I pay now for the years I did not use it?"

"I don't think it goes away, Papá." She was still reading. "It says the penalty is for as long as you have the coverage."

He was quiet for a moment. "For the rest of my life? Because I waited two years?"

"Maybe," Renata said. "But I want to check something first. There might be a reason they got it wrong, or a program that helps. Let me find out before we just accept this."

Renata was right to pause. A penalty letter is not always the final word, and even when the penalty is real, it is not always as final as it looks. This chapter is about what the letter actually means, how the three penalties are calculated, how long each one lasts, and what a family can do once the window has already closed. Some of those answers are better than families fear.

Who Actually Calculates the Penalty

One point must be clear before any of the numbers. A family never calculates its own penalty and never owes a figure it works out at the kitchen table. The penalty is determined solely by the government, by the Social Security Administration and the Centers for Medicare and Medicaid Services, using their own records of when the parent was eligible and when the parent enrolled. Every number and every method in this chapter is for education only, so that a family can understand the letter it receives, check whether it looks right, and know when to question it. The official figure always comes from the agency, not from this book, and not even from a seasoned Medicare agent, because no one outside Social Security and Medicare has the authority to set the number.

The Three Penalties at a Glance

Medicare has exactly three late enrollment penalties, one for each part that can carry one. They work differently from each other, and two differences matter most. The first is how long each penalty lasts on its own: the Part A penalty is finite and ends after a set number of years, while the Part B and Part D penalties are permanent and last for as long as the parent holds that coverage. The second is that none of the three is truly beyond relief. All three can be removed or absorbed by the safety-net programs, because Medicaid and a Medicare Savings Program can pay the Part A and

Part B premiums, penalty included, and Extra Help erases the Part D penalty outright. So the honest summary is this: one penalty ends by itself, two last for life, and all three can be lifted by the right program. Here is the shape of all three together.

Table 14.1 The three Medicare late enrollment penalties

Penalty	How it is calculated	How long it lasts
Part A late penalty	10 percent added to the Part A premium, a flat amount regardless of how many years late	For twice the number of years the parent delayed, then it ends
Part B late penalty	10 percent added for each full 12-month period the parent delayed	Permanent, for as long as the parent has Part B
Part D late penalty	1 percent of the national base beneficiary premium for each full month without creditable drug coverage	Permanent, for as long as the parent has Part D

The table shows how each penalty behaves on its own. It does not show relief. As the rest of this chapter explains, all three penalties can still be lifted by Medicaid, a Medicare Savings Program, or Extra Help for a parent who qualifies.

The Part A Penalty, and the Parent Who Never Faces It

Start with the most important exception in this whole chapter. A parent with forty work credits never faces a Part A penalty, ever, even if they miss their Part A enrollment window completely. Because their Part A is premium-free and earned through work, they can enroll in Part A whenever they choose, at any time, with no penalty at all. For these parents, the Part A deadline simply does not carry a cost.

That freedom applies to Part A only. It does not extend to Part B or Part D. A parent with forty credits who delays Part A pays nothing for the delay, but if that same parent delays Part B or Part D, the penalties for those two parts still apply in full and still last for life. The earned-credit protection covers one part and one part only.

The Part A penalty itself applies only to parents who must buy into Part A because they lack the forty-credit record. For them, the penalty is 10 percent added to the monthly Part A premium. It does not grow with the length of the delay. Whether the parent was one year late or five years late, the penalty is the same flat 10 percent. As with the other parts, only full twelve-month periods of delay count, so a parent who was eleven months late crosses no threshold and a parent who was thirteen months late is counted as one year, not more.

What changes with the length of the delay is how long the penalty lasts. The parent pays the 10 percent for twice the number of years they delayed. A parent who was two years late pays the penalty for four years, and then it disappears entirely. This is the one penalty in Medicare that ends on its own.

The Part B Penalty

The Part B penalty is the one that does the most lasting damage, because it never ends. For each full twelve-month period the parent could have enrolled but did not, 10 percent is added to the Part B premium. The penalty is then charged every month for as long as the parent has Part B, which for most parents means for life.

Two details decide how large it is. First, only full twelve-month periods count. A parent who was eleven months late pays no penalty at all, because the delay did not complete a full year. A parent who was twenty-six months late pays for two full periods, not three, because twenty-six months contains two complete years and a leftover of two months that does not reach a third. The line between one penalty tier and the next is a full twelve months, not a partial one.

Second, the penalty is calculated on the base Part B premium, not on the parent's actual premium. For a higher-income parent who pays an income-related surcharge, the penalty is figured against the standard base first, then added on top of their surcharged premium. The surcharge itself does not enlarge the penalty. Income-related surcharges are explained in the Appendix, Medicare 101 Reference.

The Part D Penalty

The third penalty attaches to prescription drug coverage, and families forget it most often because it does not involve hospital or doctor coverage. The Part D initial enrollment period is the same seven-month window as the rest of Medicare: the three months before the birthday month, the birthday month, and the three months after. After that window, the penalty is triggered by a specific gap. A parent who goes 63 or more continuous days without creditable drug coverage, at any time after the initial enrollment period ends, and then later signs up for Part D, will owe the penalty. The 63-day gap is the trigger, and it is worth watching closely, because it is short and easy to cross without noticing when other coverage ends.

The penalty is 1 percent of the national base beneficiary premium for each full month the parent went without creditable coverage. In 2026, the national base beneficiary premium is $38.99. The penalty is permanent, riding on the Part D premium for as long as the parent has drug coverage. Because it is tied to a national base that changes each year, the dollar amount shifts annually even though the percentage is locked in by the length of the original gap.

One relief is unique to Part D and worth knowing now. A parent who qualifies for Extra Help, the Part D Low Income Subsidy, does not pay the Part D penalty at all. Qualifying for Extra Help erases it for as long as the parent qualifies. This is covered with the other cost-relief programs later in the book.

A Worked Example, for Illustration Only

Numbers make the penalties concrete in a way that rules cannot. The following example uses invented premium figures, not real Medicare amounts, so the arithmetic is easy to follow. It is for illustration only. Remember that only the government calculates a real penalty. Do not use these figures for planning, and confirm real premiums against current Medicare sources.

Suppose a parent was eligible starting in 2020 but did not enroll in Part A, Part B, or Part D for twenty-four months. A twenty-four-month gap is exactly two full twelve-month periods. For Part A, this means a flat 10 percent, applied for twice the delay, which is four years. For Part B, it means 20 percent, applied for life. For Part D, twenty-four uncovered months means 24 percent, applied for life. Assume enrollment finally happens in 2022, so the penalties begin in 2022. The imaginary premiums for each year are as follows.

Note: these premium figures are invented for illustration only and are not real Medicare amounts.

Table 14.2 Invented base premiums used for the illustration

Year	Part A base premium	Part B base premium	Part D base premium
2020	100	50	10
2021	200	100	20
2022	300	150	30
2023	400	200	40
2024	500	250	50
2025	600	300	60

The first thing to notice is that the 2020 and 2021 premiums never enter the penalty math. They matter only for counting the twenty-four-month gap. The penalty is always figured on the premium of the year it is being charged, not on the premium of the year the delay happened. This is the single most common mistake families make when they try to estimate a penalty.

The Part B penalty is 20 percent of each year's base premium, charged every month, beginning in 2022.

Note: these premium figures are invented for illustration only and are not real Medicare amounts.

Table 14.3 Part B penalty in the illustration, at 20 percent

Year	Part B base	Penalty at 20 percent	Penalty per month
2022	150	150 × 0.20	30
2023	200	200 × 0.20	40
2024	250	250 × 0.20	50
2025	300	300 × 0.20	60

The Part D penalty is 24 percent of each year's base premium, charged every month, also beginning in 2022.

Note: these premium figures are invented for illustration only and are not real Medicare amounts.

Table 14.4 Part D penalty in the illustration, at 24 percent

Year	Part D base	Penalty at 24 percent	Penalty per month, rounded to nearest $0.10
2022	30	30 × 0.24 = 7.20	7.2
2023	40	40 × 0.24 = 9.60	9.6
2024	50	50 × 0.24 = 12.00	12
2025	60	60 × 0.24 = 14.40	14.4

The Part D penalty follows one rule that the other penalties do not. By law, the monthly Part D penalty is rounded to the nearest ten cents before it is added to the premium. In the table above, the figures already land on exact dimes, because the invented base numbers are round, so the rounding changes nothing here. With real numbers, it usually does. Take the actual 2026 national base beneficiary premium of $38.99. A parent with a 14 percent penalty would owe $38.99 times 0.14, which is $5.4586. Rounded to the nearest ten cents, that becomes $5.50, and $5.50 is the amount added to the monthly premium. This rounding step is small, but it is the official method, and a family checking a penalty letter should expect the Part D figure to be rounded this way.

The Part A penalty is a flat 10 percent, applied for four years only, which here means 2022 through 2025.

Note: these premium figures are invented for illustration only and are not real Medicare amounts.

Table 14.5 Part A penalty in the illustration, at 10 percent

Year	Part A base	Penalty at 10 percent	Penalty per month
2022	300	300 × 0.10	30
2023	400	400 × 0.10	40
2024	500	500 × 0.10	50
2025	600	600 × 0.10	60

After 2025, the Part A penalty ends because four years have passed. From 2026 onward, the parent pays only the base Part A premium with no penalty. This is the difference in the penalties made visible. The Part A column stops. The Part B and Part D columns never do.

What the Real Premiums Looked Like

The example above used round invented numbers so the arithmetic stayed clear. The real premiums are messier, and it helps to see them, because they show the true dollar scale a penalty attaches to. The table below lists the actual figures for recent years. The Part A premium shown is the full buy-in rate for a parent with fewer than thirty quarters of work, since a parent with forty credits pays nothing for Part A. The Part B figure is the standard monthly premium, and the Part D figure is the national base beneficiary premium that the Part D penalty is calculated from.

These are real Medicare figures for the years shown.

Table 14.6 Real Medicare base premiums, recent years

Year	Part A full buy-in premium	Part B standard premium	Part D national base premium
2020	458	144.6	32.74
2021	471	148.5	33.06
2022	499	170.1	33.37
2023	506	164.9	32.74
2024	505	174.7	34.7
2025	518	185	36.78

These real figures make the trend honest. Over time, the premiums clearly move upward, and the direction across the years is unmistakable. But the rise is not perfectly smooth. There are exceptions. The Part B premium fell in 2023, dropping from $170.10 to $164.90. The Part A buy-in dipped by a dollar in 2024. The Part D base fell in 2023 before climbing again. The lesson for a family is not that premiums rise every single year without fail, but that they trend upward strongly over time despite the occasional dip. A permanent penalty, set as a percentage, therefore grows in dollar terms across the years even when a single year happens to fall, because the penalty tracks whatever the base is in each year.

How to Undo a Penalty

A penalty letter is not always the final word. There are three routes to deal with one, and they serve different situations.

The first route is equitable relief. This applies when the parent enrolled late because a government employee gave wrong or misleading information, or failed to act. If a Social Security representative told a family the wrong deadline, or an official process delayed the enrollment, the family can request equitable relief to have the penalty reduced or removed. There is no formal appeal if equitable relief is denied, but there is also no limit on resubmitting the request with more or better information. Families should document every interaction with a government office, because that documentation is what supports the request.

The second route is a reconsideration appeal. This applies when the family believes the penalty itself was calculated wrongly, for example when the parent actually had creditable coverage during the months Medicare counted as a gap. For Part B, the family follows the instructions on the penalty letter or uses Social Security's reconsideration request. For Part D, there is a specific reconsideration request form, and the appeal must be filed within sixty days of the penalty notice. Appeals after sixty days are considered only if there was a valid reason for the delay.

The third route is qualifying for a cost-relief program. This is not an appeal and does not depend on proving anyone made a mistake. A parent who qualifies for a Medicare Savings Program, or for full Medicaid, can have the Part A and Part B premiums paid on their behalf, which absorbs the Part A and Part B penalties along with them, because each penalty is part of the premium it rides on. A parent who qualifies for Extra Help, the Part D Low Income Subsidy, has the Part D penalty erased entirely for as long as they qualify. This means every one of the three penalties can be lifted through the safety net, not only the Part D penalty. For a family facing a permanent penalty they cannot appeal away, this route is often the most powerful of the three. These programs, who qualifies and how to apply, are covered in Chapter 18 as part of the money safety net.

The honest picture is that none of the three routes is guaranteed. Equitable relief depends on proving government error, appeals depend on proving the calculation was wrong, and cost-relief programs depend on the parent's income and assets. But families often accept a penalty they could have challenged or offset, simply because the letter looked final. It is not.

Action Checklist

- ☐ Remember that only the government calculates a real penalty. Use this chapter to understand and check the letter, not to compute an official figure.
- ☐ Identify which of the three penalties the parent faces: Part A, Part B, Part D, or more than one at once.
- ☐ If the parent has forty work credits, know that Part A carries no penalty ever, even if the Part A window was missed. This protection does not extend to Part B or Part D.
- ☐ For the Part A penalty, remember it is a flat 10 percent and lasts only twice the number of years delayed, then ends. Only full twelve-month periods count.
- ☐ For the Part B penalty, count only full twelve-month periods of delay. Eleven months is no penalty, and twenty-six months is two periods, not three.
- ☐ For Part D, watch the 63-day rule. A gap of 63 or more continuous days without creditable drug coverage after the initial enrollment period triggers the penalty. Note the Part D penalty is rounded to the nearest ten cents.
- ☐ Remember the Part B and Part D penalties are permanent and recalculated each year against a base that trends upward over time, so the dollar cost grows across the years.
- ☐ Remember too that all three penalties can be lifted for a parent who qualifies for Medicaid, a Medicare Savings Program, or Extra Help. A permanent penalty is not always a permanent cost.
- ☐ If the late enrollment was caused by wrong information from a government office, request equitable relief and document every interaction. There is no limit on resubmitting.

- ☐ If the penalty count looks wrong because the parent had creditable coverage, file a reconsideration appeal. For Part D, use the reconsideration request form within sixty days of the notice.
- ☐ Check eligibility for Extra Help and Medicare Savings Programs, which can erase the Part D penalty and absorb the Part A and Part B premiums and penalties. See Chapter 18.
- ☐ Verify every penalty figure and relief rule against current Medicare sources, because base premiums and the national base beneficiary premium change every year.

CHAPTER 15

Dignity I
Foundation: Building on Medicare

"So she's enrolled," Ama said. "Part A, Part B, everything went through. We're done, right?"

The counselor smiled and shook her head gently. "You're enrolled. That's the hard part, and you did it on time. But enrolling is not the same as being covered the way you'll want to be. Right now your father has the frame of a house. No walls yet."

Ama frowned. "I thought Part A and Part B were the coverage."

"They're the foundation. They pay most hospital and doctor bills. But they leave twenty percent of the doctor side on your father, with no ceiling, and they don't cover his prescriptions at all. So there's a decision to make now, and it's the biggest one after enrollment itself. How do you want to build on the foundation?"

Ama had helped her father, Mr. Osei, cross the enrollment finish line in the last chapter. She thought that was the end. It was actually the beginning of the part that shapes what he pays and what he is protected from for the rest of his life. This is the foundation layer of the three layers of dignity, and it starts with a single choice that everything else rests on.

Why the Foundation Is a Choice, Not a Default

Original Medicare, Part A and Part B together, is real coverage, but it was never designed to stand alone. It pays about eighty percent of the cost of covered doctor and outpatient services after the deductible, and it leaves the other twenty percent to the beneficiary. That twenty percent has no annual limit. There is no cap, no maximum, no point at which Original Medicare says the year's out-of-pocket cost is enough. A single serious illness can turn that open-ended twenty percent into a very large number. And Original Medicare does not cover most prescription drugs at all. That is why the foundation is a choice. A family has to decide how to close those two gaps, the twenty percent and the drugs, and the way they close them defines the rest of the plan.

The Three Combinations That Keep a Family Penalty-Safe

There are only three combinations that protect a parent from every type of Medicare penalty while giving them working coverage. Every family should hold one of them. Each one is complete in the sense that it closes the drug gap and avoids the penalties, but they differ in how they cover care and in what they cost. Here they are.

Table 15.1 The three penalty-safe coverage combinations

Combination	What it is	What it protects against
1. Part A + Part B + Part D	Original Medicare plus a standalone drug plan	Penalty-safe on all parts, but the 20 percent doctor-side coinsurance stays on the parent with no cap
2. Part A + Part B + Part C	Original Medicare delivered through a Medicare Advantage plan, which usually includes Part D	Penalty-safe, adds an out-of-pocket cap, and usually bundles drugs and extra benefits
3. Part A + Part B + Part D + Medigap	Original Medicare plus a drug plan plus a Medicare Supplement policy	Penalty-safe and closes most of the 20 percent gap, the strongest protection, at the highest cost

One rule sits underneath the table and is worth stating plainly. A parent must enroll in Part A and Part B first in every case. Part C, Part D, and Medigap all build on top of Part A and Part B. They are not substitutes for enrolling. This is why enrollment had to come first, back in Chapter 13. Without the foundation, none of these three combinations exist.

A second rule matters just as much. Combinations Two and Three cannot be mixed. A parent cannot hold a Medicare Advantage plan and a Medigap policy at the same time. Medigap is designed to fill the gaps in Original Medicare, and a Medicare Advantage plan replaces the way Original Medicare delivers those benefits, so the two do not work together, and it is not legal to sell a parent both. A family chooses one road or the other.

Combination One: The Bare Minimum

The first combination is Original Medicare with a standalone Part D drug plan. It keeps the parent fully penalty-safe, because Part D is in place and the drug gap is closed. For a family with a parent in good health, it is a legitimate floor.

Its weakness is the twenty percent. Under this combination, the parent still owes twenty percent of the cost of every covered doctor and outpatient service, and there is no annual ceiling on that amount. A year of good health costs little. A year with surgery, cancer treatment, or a long series of specialist visits can cost far more than a family expects, because the twenty percent keeps running with no stop. This combination protects against penalties. It does not protect against a catastrophic medical year. A family choosing it should understand that they are accepting that open-ended risk.

Combination Two: The Balanced Choice

The second combination is Medicare Advantage, known as Part C. The parent stays enrolled in Part A and Part B, and a private plan approved by Medicare delivers those benefits, usually with prescription drug coverage built in, so the family does not buy a separate Part D plan. For most seniors, this is the most affordable path to broad coverage. About three-quarters of Advantage enrollees in plans that include drug coverage pay no premium beyond the Part B premium they already pay, and across all Advantage plans the average premium in 2026 is only about fourteen dollars a month. Because the drug coverage is built in, and because plans often negotiate lower drug costs, many families find their total monthly cost lower on this road than they expect.

What makes it balanced is what comes with it. Most Advantage plans add benefits Original Medicare never included, commonly dental, vision, hearing, and fitness memberships, and they carry a legal out-of-pocket maximum. The law caps the in-network maximum at $9,250 in 2026, but that is only the ceiling, and most plans sit well below it. The average in-network out-of-pocket maximum for Advantage enrollees in 2026 is about $5,421, far lower than the legal limit. Once the parent reaches their plan's cap, the plan pays the rest for the year. That cap is exactly what Combination One lacks, and it is a large part of why many families find Advantage the most sensible balance of cost and protection.

One feature inside Medicare Advantage is easy to miss and worth naming. Some Advantage plans, known as Part B giveback plans, pay back a portion of the parent's Part B premium, and in some cases all of it. About a quarter of Advantage plans offer this in 2026. The plan rebates part of the $202.90 Part B premium, which raises the parent's Social Security payment by that amount, since the premium is what gets deducted from the check. These plans are not available everywhere, and the giveback never exceeds the Part B premium itself, but for a budget-conscious family in an area where they are offered, a giveback plan can lower the true monthly cost of coverage further still.

The honest tradeoff is how Advantage plans manage care. They generally use provider networks, so a parent may need to stay with doctors and hospitals in the plan, and they often require prior authorization for certain services. For a parent who travels, who wants any doctor anywhere, or who has complex conditions requiring many specialists, those limits matter and should be weighed. For many parents, the extra benefits and the cap outweigh the network limits, but the fit is individual, which is exactly where a good agent earns their place.

Combination Three: The Strongest Protection

The third combination is Original Medicare, a standalone Part D drug plan, and a Medigap policy, also called a Medicare Supplement. Medigap is private insurance whose only job is to pay the costs Original Medicare leaves behind, most importantly that twenty percent. With a strong Medigap policy, the parent can see almost any doctor who accepts Medicare, anywhere in the country, with little or nothing owed at the point of care and no network to stay inside. This is the most complete and the most flexible protection of the three.

It is also the most expensive, and the cost has a shape a family must understand. Medigap is a separate monthly premium on top of Part B and Part D, and with the common attained-age pricing, that premium rises as the parent grows older. It can look affordable at sixty-five and become steep at eighty. A family choosing Combination Three is buying the strongest coverage and the greatest freedom, and paying for it with a premium that starts higher than the others and climbs over time. For a parent who can afford it and who values seeing any doctor without gatekeeping, it is often worth every dollar. For a family on a tight budget, the rising cost is a real consideration. And because Medigap cannot be combined with Medicare Advantage, choosing this road means choosing it instead of Combination Two, not alongside it.

Special Needs Plans, a Better Fit for Some Parents

The three combinations cover most families, but there is a category inside Medicare Advantage built for specific situations, called Special Needs Plans. They are still Part C plans, so they carry the same penalty-safe protection and the same out-of-pocket cap, but they are designed and priced for parents who meet certain conditions. Two of them matter most for the families in this book.

The first is the Chronic Condition Special Needs Plan, or C-SNP. This plan is limited to people who have a qualifying severe or chronic condition, such as diabetes, chronic heart failure, or a lung disorder. For a parent living with a serious ongoing illness, a C-SNP tailors its drug list, its provider network, and its care coordination around that condition. It is often a stronger fit than a general Advantage plan for a parent whose health is dominated by one major diagnosis, because the whole plan is organized around managing it.

The second, and the more powerful for a low-income immigrant parent, is the Dual Eligible Special Needs Plan, or D-SNP. This plan is only for parents who have both Medicare and Medicaid at the same time. That dual eligibility is the entry requirement, so a parent must first qualify for Medicaid to join one. For those who do qualify, a D-SNP is remarkably generous. Cost sharing is typically minimal or nothing, so copayments and coinsurance largely disappear, and the plan usually adds benefits well beyond a standard Advantage plan, commonly a monthly grocery or healthy-food allowance, over-the-counter product money, and transportation to medical visits. For a parent who is dual eligible, a D-SNP can turn a tight medical budget into one that is nearly fully covered, with real help for daily needs on top

Because a D-SNP depends on qualifying for Medicaid, it connects directly to the money safety net. A family whose parent might qualify for Medicaid should read Chapter 18, which covers how Medicaid and the related programs work, and then ask whether a D-SNP is available in their area. For a dual-eligible parent, it is often the single best coverage choice on the board.

How to Think About the Choice

Do not mistake the three combinations for a ranking from worst to best. They are simply three honest answers to different situations. Combination One fits a healthy parent whose family can accept open-ended risk in exchange for the simplest setup. Combination Two fits the largest number of parents, offering broad coverage, extra benefits, and a spending cap at low cost, in exchange for networks and prior authorization. Combination Three fits a parent who wants maximum freedom and protection and can carry a premium that rises with age. No combination is right for everyone, and the wrong question is which is best in the abstract. The right question is which fits this parent, this health, and this budget. And for some parents the best answer is not a general plan at all but a Special Needs Plan, a C-SNP for a parent with a serious chronic illness, or a D-SNP for a parent who also has Medicaid.

This is the decision where a knowledgeable Medicare agent is most valuable. A good agent does three things here. They match the combination to the parent's health, budget, and doctors. They screen out plans that look attractive but fit poorly, or that are sold aggressively without regard for the parent's situation. And they coordinate the pieces so drug coverage, supplemental coverage, and the foundation all line up without a gap or a penalty. The choice is the family's to make. The agent's job is to make sure it is an informed one. See Chapter 19 for how to find and work with an agent.

The next two chapters build the layers that sit on this foundation. Chapter 16 takes up the second layer of dignity, the supplemental plans that add protection for specific risks like cancer, critical illness, hospital stays, and dementia, and how they work alongside Medicare Advantage and Medigap. Chapter 17 takes up the third layer, long-term care. Both rest on the foundation chosen here.

Action Checklist

- ☐ Confirm the parent is enrolled in Part A and Part B first. Every combination builds on that foundation.

☐ Understand that Original Medicare alone leaves a 20 percent co-insurance with no annual cap and does not cover most drugs. The foundation must be built on.

☐ Choose one of the three penalty-safe combinations: Original Medicare plus Part D, Medicare Advantage that includes Part D, or Original Medicare plus Part D plus Medigap.

☐ Remember that Medicare Advantage and Medigap cannot be held together. Choosing one rules out the other.

☐ For Combination One, accept that the simple setup comes with open-ended 20 percent risk in a bad health year.

☐ For Combination Two, weigh the low cost, the out-of-pocket cap, and extra benefits against provider networks and prior authorization. Note that most 2026 plans sit well below the $9,250 legal ceiling, averaging about $5,421 in-network, and about three-quarters of drug-inclusive plans charge no premium beyond Part B.

☐ Ask whether a Part B giveback plan is offered in the parent's area. About a quarter of 2026 Advantage plans rebate part, and sometimes all, of the Part B premium, though availability varies by location.

☐ Consider a Special Needs Plan where it fits. A C-SNP suits a parent with a serious chronic condition, and a D-SNP suits a parent who has both Medicare and Medicaid, usually with minimal cost sharing and extras like a grocery allowance. See Chapter 18 for Medicaid eligibility.

☐ For Combination Three, weigh the strongest, most flexible coverage against a premium that starts higher and rises with age under attained-age pricing.

☐ Match the choice to the parent's health, budget, and preferred doctors, not to which plan sounds best in general.

☐ Involve a Medicare agent to match, screen, and coordinate the pieces. See Chapter 19.

- ☐ Verify all plan details, premiums, and current out-of-pocket figures against current Medicare sources, because these change every year.

CHAPTER 16

Dignity Protection: Coverage That Pays You Money

[illegible]

[illegible]

[illegible]

Dignity II
Protection: Coverage That Pays You Money

Ama and her friend Lucia had not talked since their fathers turned sixty-five within a few months of each other. Over coffee, the conversation went where it always went now, to their parents.

"We picked the Advantage plan for my dad," Ama said. "The one with the dental and the low premium. But I keep thinking about those hospital copays, a few hundred dollars a day if he's admitted. Did we leave him exposed?"

"We went the other way," Lucia said. "My father sees three specialists and didn't want to think about networks at all, so we chose Medigap. Higher premium, but there's almost nothing left for Medicare to leave him holding. I figured that meant we were done."

"So you didn't add anything on top."

"That's what I thought. But we did add one thing, a critical illness plan. The Medigap pays the hospital. What it doesn't pay for is everything around a serious diagnosis, me taking time off work, a ramp for the front steps, a driver to treatment. The plan hands us cash for that."

Ama sat back. "That's the part I've been circling. We're not paying a Medigap premium at all. I keep wondering what we should do with the money we're not spending."

The two of them arrived at the same thought at once. They had chosen two different foundations, Mr. Osei on Medicare Advantage, Mr. Reyes on Medigap. And each of them was building, or needed to build, the same second story on top: a layer of coverage that pays the family in cash, for the things the foundation was never designed to reach.

This is the protection layer, the second of the three layers of dignity. The foundation in Chapter 15 decides how care is delivered and what the big structure covers. The second layer decides what happens in the gaps, and it is built differently depending on which foundation a family chose, but for every family it does something the foundation alone cannot: it puts cash in the family's hands when illness strikes.

What Supplemental Plans Are

Supplemental plans are a different kind of insurance from the foundation. They do not pay doctors and hospitals directly the way Medicare or Medigap does. Instead, they pay cash, either a fixed amount for a specific event or a lump sum on a specific diagnosis, and that cash goes to the family to use however they choose. Three kinds matter most for a senior building this layer.

A hospital indemnity plan pays a fixed cash amount for each day, or each event, of a covered hospital stay. If a parent is admitted and the Advantage plan charges a daily copay for the first several days, the hospital indemnity plan pays a set amount that can match or exceed that copay. It is aimed squarely at the gap Medicare Advantage leaves in the hospital.

A critical illness plan pays a lump sum of cash when the parent is diagnosed with a covered serious condition, commonly a heart attack, stroke, or kidney failure. A cancer plan does the same for a cancer diagnosis. The money arrives as a single payment and belongs to the family, to spend on treatment costs, on bills, or on anything the illness makes necessary.

A dementia plan pays a benefit upon a diagnosis of dementia or a similar cognitive condition. This is the thinnest of the supplemental products, and it must be understood honestly. A dementia supplemental plan can provide a helpful cash benefit, but it does not carry the weight of what dementia actually costs, which is long-term care over years. That larger problem is the subject of Chapter 17, the third layer. Here, a dementia plan is one modest tool, not the answer to dementia's real expense.

The Strategy That Changes Everything

Here is the move that most families never hear, and it is the center of this chapter for a family on Medicare Advantage. A parent who chose Advantage is not paying a Medigap premium. Medigap, the strongest road in Chapter 15, costs a monthly premium that starts high and climbs with age. The Advantage road usually costs little or nothing beyond the Part B premium. That difference is real money, month after month, and a family can decide to spend it rather than simply pocket it.

Spent well, that money buys supplemental plans that fill the very gaps Advantage leaves. Hospital indemnity covers the daily hospital copays. A critical illness or cancer plan covers the lump-cost shock of a major diagnosis. Layered together, these plans close the middle zone that sits beneath the Advantage out-of-pocket cap, the zone Ama worried about. In effect, the family uses the money Medigap would have cost to bring the Advantage plan's protection up toward the level Medigap would have provided.

And this is where the strategy does something Medigap alone cannot. The parent still has the Advantage extras, the dental, vision, hearing, and fitness benefits that Medigap never offers. So the family ends up with protection approaching Medigap's, plus the everyday benefits Medigap has no version of. For many families, this is a better use of the same dollars than buying Medigap outright.

One honest note keeps this accurate. Supplemental plans pay on specific triggers, a hospital day, a covered diagnosis so they fill gaps in a targeted way rather than covering every last dollar of the twenty percent the way Medigap does automatically. The strategy provides a family with a very close and smart approximation of Medigap, rather than an identical copy. A family should build the layer with that understanding.

When the Cash Becomes More Than Gap-Filling

There is a second use of this layer that goes beyond matching Medigap, and it is the part families find most surprising. Because supplemental plans pay cash directly to the family, a parent who layers them generously ends up with money in hand precisely when a serious illness strikes. That cash does not have to go to a medical bill. It can go to the expenses of illness that no medical plan, not Medicare, not Advantage, not Medigap, ever covers.

Those expenses are real, and they are often what breaks a family financially. Family support, when an adult child takes unpaid time from work to care for a parent. A recovery cushion, to carry the household through months of reduced income. Home modifications, a ramp, a walk-in shower, a stair lift, to let the parent stay home. Transportation and lodging, when treatment is far away, and a family must travel and stay. Household help, cleaning, cooking, and errands the parent can no longer manage alone. Medigap pays a hospital bill. It does not put cash in a family's hands for any of this. A well-built second layer does exactly that.

How the Layer Changes with the Foundation

The second layer is built differently depending on which foundation the family chose in Chapter 15, and this is where the layering has to be matched with care. Neither foundation is the better one; each simply asks the second layer to do a different job.

For a parent on Medicare Advantage, the second layer does the most work. It fills the daily hospital copays, it cushions the exposure up to the out-of-pocket cap, and it delivers the cash described above. This is the pairing that turns a low-premium plan into strong, cash-rich protection, and it is the case where the strategy of redirecting the Medigap money applies in full.

For a parent on Medigap, the second layer does less gap-filling, and a family should not over-buy. Medigap already closes most of the twenty percent automatically, so hospital indemnity and copay-filling plans are largely redundant on top of it. What still has value for a Medigap parent is the pure cash protection, a critical illness or cancer lump sum, or a dementia benefit, used not to fill medical gaps but to fund the lifestyle and care expenses that Medigap never touches. A Medigap family should buy the second layer for the cash, not for gap-filling they already have. This is exactly what Lucia's family did for Mr. Reyes.

The Agent's Role in Building the Layer

This layer is easy to build badly. There are many supplemental products, some sold aggressively, some priced poorly, some overlapping in ways that waste a family's money. A knowledgeable agent matters here for the same three reasons as in the foundation chapter. They match the supplemental plans to the parent's health, budget, and foundation, so an Advantage parent gets the gap-filling they need and a Medigap parent is not sold coverage they already have. They screen out weak or predatory products and needless overlap. And they coordinate the pieces so the second layer sits correctly on the foundation without duplication or holes. The choices belong to the family. The agent makes sure the layer is built to fit, not sold piece by piece. See Chapter 19 for how to find and work with an agent.

The third layer, long-term care, sits on top of everything built here, and it carries the highest cost of all, including the full weight of dementia care that this chapter only touched. That is Chapter 17.

Action Checklist

- ☐ Understand the second layer pays cash, not providers. Hospital indemnity pays per hospital day or event, critical illness and cancer plans pay a lump sum on diagnosis, and a dementia plan pays a limited benefit on diagnosis.
- ☐ If the parent chose Medicare Advantage, consider redirecting the money a Medigap premium would have cost into supplemental plans that fill the daily hospital copays and the exposure under the out-of-pocket cap.
- ☐ Recognize that this strategy brings Advantage protection close to Medigap while keeping the dental, vision, hearing, and fitness benefits Medigap never offers, though it approximates Medigap rather than copying it exactly.

- ☐ Consider layering beyond gap-filling so the cash can fund the real expenses of illness that no medical plan covers: family support, a recovery cushion, home modifications, transportation and lodging, and household help.
- ☐ If the parent chose Medigap, do not over-buy. Most copay-filling plans are redundant on top of Medigap. Buy the second layer for the cash lump sums, not for gaps Medigap already closes.
- ☐ Treat dementia coverage here as one limited tool only. The full cost of dementia care is long-term care, covered in Chapter 17.
- ☐ Involve a Medicare agent to match, screen, and coordinate the layer to the parent's foundation and budget. See Chapter 19.
- ☐ Verify every product's triggers, benefit amounts, and exclusions before buying, because supplemental plans vary widely and pay only on their specific covered events.

Part Five · The Three Layers of Dignity

Chapter 17

Dignity III
Legacy: Planning for Long-Term Care

Ama's father was doing well. It was her neighbor's mother, Grace, who had changed everything for the family next door, and Ama had watched it happen over the fence.

"The hospital was covered," the neighbor told her one evening. "The Medicare part worked exactly like it was supposed to. She had the rehab, the hundred days, all of it. And then the hundred days ended, and she still couldn't be left alone, and someone from the facility sat us down and told us Medicare doesn't pay for this part. The part where she just needs help living. That's on us."

"How much is it?" Ama asked.

"Almost $8,000 a month for the memory unit. I did the math on the drive home. In a year, that's most of what my parents saved in their whole lives. We're going to spend it all, and then something called Medicaid takes over, and I still don't fully understand how."

This is the third layer, the legacy layer, and it is the one families understand the least and fear the most. The foundation in Chapter 15 pays the doctor and the hospital. The second layer in Chapter 16 puts cash in the family's hands when illness strikes. Neither of them pays for long-term care, the ongoing help with daily living that a parent may need for years, and that is the single largest financial risk a senior faces. This chapter is about facing it on purpose, before the day someone from a facility sits the family down.

What Long-Term Care Is, and Why Medicare Does Not Cover It

Long-term care is help with the ordinary activities of daily living, bathing, dressing, eating, moving from a bed to a chair, using the bathroom, when a person can no longer manage them alone. It is not medical treatment in the usual sense. No one is curing anything. The parent simply needs another person's help to get through the day, sometimes for months, often for years.

This is the care Medicare does not pay for, and the gap surprises almost every family. Medicare covers a short, skilled stay, up to one hundred days in a benefit period, when a parent needs actual skilled nursing or rehabilitation, usually after a hospital stay. Once the skilled need ends, or the hundred days run out, Medicare stops. The kind of help Grace needed, called custodial care, is not covered at all, no matter how long it lasts or how much it costs. Neither Medigap nor a Medicare Advantage plan fills this gap, because both are built on top of Medicare and follow the same rule.

So a family that has done everything right in the first two layers- enrolled on time, chosen a foundation, built a cash layer- can still be completely unprotected against the largest cost of all. That is why this third layer has to be planned separately.

What Long-Term Care Actually Costs

The numbers are the reason this chapter exists. According to the CareScout 2025 Cost of Care Survey, the most recent national survey of its kind, the median cost of assisted living is about $6,200 a month, roughly $74,400 a year. A semi-private room in a nursing home runs a national median near $9,600 a month, about $115,000 a year, and a private room exceeds $129,000 a year. Memory care is harder to pin to a single figure, because it is not tracked as its own national category, but estimates commonly range from about $7,000 to well over $10,000 a month depending on the region and the level of care. In higher-cost states, every one of these numbers is substantially larger, and care at home with an aide for many hours a day can cost as much as a facility.

These figures are national medians for illustration, and a family should check the real cost in its own area, because local prices vary widely. But the shape of the problem is the same everywhere. A single year of memory care can consume most of what an ordinary family saved across a working lifetime, and long-term care is rarely a single year. This is a cost large enough to erase an estate, which is exactly why the third layer is called the legacy layer. What is protected here is not only the parent's care but whatever the parent hoped to leave behind.

The Three Ways Families Pay for Long-Term Care

There are only three real ways to pay for long-term care, and most families end up using some combination of them. The choice a family makes ahead of time determines which one it leans on, and how much of the parent's savings survives.

The first way is to pay out of pocket. The family simply spends the parent's savings and income on care as it is needed. For a short stay, this is manageable. For a long one, it is how an estate disappears, month by month, until little or nothing is left. Paying out of pocket is what happens by default to a family that made no other plan.

The second way is private insurance bought in advance, and it comes in two forms. A standalone long-term care insurance policy pays a daily or monthly benefit toward care once the parent needs help with a set number of daily activities. It is the most direct tool, but it must be bought while the parent is still healthy enough to qualify, and its premiums can rise over time. A hybrid policy combines long-term care coverage with life insurance or an annuity. It costs more up front, often a single large premium or a set number of payments, but it solves the complaint families have about standalone policies: that the money is lost if the care is never needed. With a hybrid, if the parent never needs long-term care, the policy still pays a death benefit to the family, so the money is not wasted either way. Both forms must be arranged years before the need, not in the middle of a crisis.

The third way is Medicaid. Unlike Medicare, Medicaid does pay for long-term custodial care, including years in a nursing home, and for many families it is the only thing standing between them and an unlimited bill. But Medicaid is a program for people with very limited assets, so a parent generally qualifies only after spending down savings to a low limit set by the state. This is what Grace's neighbor was describing: the estate spent almost to nothing, and then Medicaid taking over. Medicaid is the safety net that catches a family at the bottom, and how a parent qualifies for it and applies is the subject of Chapter 18, where it sits alongside the other safety-net programs.

The Last Gift: Planning for Final Expenses

When Ama's aunt passed, the grief was hard enough. What made it harder was the week that followed: the phone calls, the estimates, the sudden question of whether the family could bring her body home to be buried beside her husband, and the quiet math no one wanted to do while the loss was still fresh. Ama watched her cousins carry that weight on top of their sorrow, and she made a decision. Whatever else she planned for her father, she would not let his passing become a scramble for the people who loved him most.

Final expenses are the one-time costs that come after a life ends: a funeral or cremation, a burial or the transport of a body home, and the small debts and paperwork that surface in the first weeks. They are not the same as long-term care. Long-term care is a large, ongoing cost while a parent is living; final expenses are a smaller, one-time cost after they are gone. Both belong to the legacy layer, but they answer different questions, and it helps to keep them apart in your mind.

This part of the plan is not about money, or not mainly. It costs far less than the care layers, and yet it may be the piece your family remembers most. A parent who has set this aside gives their children something precise and merciful: the freedom to grieve without a bill in their hands. Instead of arguments about what Mom would have wanted, there is an answer. Instead of a sudden expense split awkwardly among siblings, there is a plan already made. That is the last gift, and it is one of the most loving things a parent can leave.

For immigrant families, there is often one more layer to think through: the wish to return a parent to their home country to be laid to rest. Repatriation can cost far more than a local service and involves paperwork across two countries, and it is not something a grieving family should be discovering for the first time at the worst moment of their lives. If this matters to your parent, it is worth naming out loud now, while there is time to plan for it calmly.

Families handle this in different ways. Some simply set aside savings marked for the purpose. Others choose a small final-expense insurance policy so the money is ready the moment it is needed. There is no single right answer, and this book does not push one. What matters is that the decision is made on purpose, in daylight, rather than left for children to face in the dark. If your family wants to weigh the options, the team in Chapter 19, including a trusted agent, can walk you through them without pressure.

Where Dementia Fits

Chapter 16 introduced a dementia supplemental plan and said plainly that it does not carry the real weight of dementia. This is where that weight lands. Dementia is, above all, a long-term care problem. A parent with advancing dementia may need years of supervision and help with daily living, often in a memory-care unit at the highest cost of any setting. Medicare will not pay for it. A dementia supplemental cash plan helps a little. What actually carries a family through years of memory care is one of the three ways above: private long-term care coverage arranged in advance, or Medicaid once savings are gone. A family with a history of dementia has the strongest possible reason to build this third layer early, while the parent is still healthy enough to qualify for private coverage.

Planning Early Is the Whole Game

The hard truth of the third layer is that almost every good option requires acting before the need arrives. A parent can only buy long-term care insurance or a hybrid policy while still healthy; once care is needed, the door to private coverage has closed. Medicaid planning, arranging a parent's finances legitimately so the family is not caught entirely unprotected, also takes time and often must be done years ahead to be effective. The family that waits until a parent needs care, like Grace's, is usually left with only the first and third ways, spending down out of pocket and then falling to Medicaid.

This does not mean every family should buy long-term care insurance. For some, the premiums do not fit the budget, and a deliberate plan to rely on Medicaid is a legitimate choice made with open eyes rather than a disaster stumbled into. The point is that the decision should be made on purpose, early, with the real numbers in front of the family, and not discovered in a facility hallway on the hundred-and-first day.

The Agent's Role in the Third Layer

Long-term care planning reaches beyond what a Medicare agent alone handles, and a family should know that. A knowledgeable agent can match and explain long-term care insurance and hybrid policies, and can tell a family honestly whether private coverage fits their budget and health. But the Medicaid side- spend-down rules and legitimate planning- is often the work of an elder-law attorney, and the estate side may involve a financial planner. The agent's honest role here is partly to build the private-insurance piece and partly to tell a family plainly when they need to bring in other professionals. A family should be wary of anyone selling a single product as the whole answer to long-term care, because it rarely is. See Chapter 19 for how to find and work with the right people.

Action Checklist

- ☐ Understand that Medicare does not pay for long-term custodial care. It covers only a short skilled stay, up to one hundred days in a benefit period, and neither Medigap nor Medicare Advantage fills this gap.

- ☐ Learn the real cost of care in the parent's own area. National medians from the CareScout 2025 Cost of Care Survey run about $6,200 a month for assisted living and roughly $9,600 a month for a semi-private nursing home room, with memory care commonly ranging from about $7,000 to well over $10,000 a month; local prices vary widely.
- ☐ Recognize the three ways to pay: out of pocket, private insurance bought in advance, or Medicaid after a spend-down. Most families use a combination.
- ☐ If considering private coverage, weigh standalone long-term care insurance against a hybrid policy that also pays a death benefit if care is never needed, and remember both must be bought while the parent is still healthy.
- ☐ Treat a family history of dementia as the strongest reason to build this layer early, because dementia is chiefly a long-term care cost and lands at the highest-priced setting.
- ☐ Plan for final expenses as part of the legacy layer: the one-time costs after a parent passes, kept separate from long-term care.
- ☐ Talk about final wishes openly now, including whether repatriation to the home country matters, so children are not deciding under grief and time pressure.
- ☐ Decide on purpose how final expenses will be met, whether through set-aside savings or a small final-expense policy, and revisit the choice as circumstances change.
- ☐ Choose purpose and early, with real numbers in hand. Deciding to rely on Medicaid is legitimate, but only when chosen with open eyes rather than discovered in a crisis.
- ☐ Bring in the right professionals. A Medicare agent can handle the private-insurance piece, but Medicaid spend-down and estate planning often call for an elder-law attorney and a financial planner. See Chapter 19.
- ☐ For how a parent qualifies for Medicaid and applies, along with MSP and Extra Help, see Chapter 18, the money safety net.

CHAPTER 18

The Programs That Pay When a Family Cannot

Marisol had a folder now. Inside it was everything about her mother's Medicare, the enrollment dates, the plan card, the penalty letter they had fought and lost. What she did not have was a way to pay for all of it on her mother's income.

"She gets a little over $1,500 a month," Marisol told the counselor. "The Part B premium comes out of that, and now the penalty on top of it. Then the drug plan. By the time the month is over, there is almost nothing left of the food. I keep thinking we did everything right and it still doesn't add up."

"You may have done everything right," the counselor said. "And there may be a door you haven't opened yet. At an income like your mother's, some programs can pay her Medicare premiums, eliminate the penalty that comes with them, and cut her drug costs to a few dollars per prescription. Most families never learn these exist. Let's find out if she qualifies."

This is the safety net, the layer beneath all the others. Everything in the earlier chapters assumed a family could pay the premiums and the costs that Medicare leaves behind. This chapter is for the families who cannot, and it carries good news that too few of them ever hear: for a parent with limited income, the government itself will step in and pay, and in doing so it can erase the very penalties that earlier chapters worked so hard to avoid.

Three Programs, One Purpose

There are three programs at the center of this chapter, and together they cover the three parts of Medicare that cost money. The Medicare Savings Programs pay the Part A and Part B premiums. Extra Help, also called the Part D Low-Income Subsidy, pays down the drug costs. And Medicaid, the largest of the three, can pay for what nothing else does, including the long-term care that Chapter 17 described. A parent may qualify for one of these, or for several at once, and the programs are built to work together.

One rule runs underneath all of them and is worth stating before the details. These are programs for people with limited income and limited assets. The federal government sets the shape of each program, and the states fill in most of the actual numbers. So every limit in this chapter is a reliable federal figure, and every family should still check its own state, because a state may use a higher limit or ignore certain income or assets entirely. Where this chapter gives a number, treat it as the floor of what is possible, not the ceiling.

The Medicare Savings Programs, and How They Erase the Part A and Part B Penalties

The Medicare Savings Programs, or MSPs, are run by each state's Medicaid office, and they pay a parent's Medicare premiums. There are four. They differ mainly by income limit and by how much they cover, as the two tables below show.

Table 18.1 - Medicare Savings Programs, What Each Pays (2026)

Program	What it pays	Late-enrollment penalty it absorbs
QMB (Qualified Medicare Beneficiary)	Part A premium (if owed) and Part B premium, plus Medicare deductibles, coinsurance, and copayments	Part A penalty (if owed) and Part B penalty
SLMB (Specified Low-Income Medicare Beneficiary)	Part B premium only	Part B penalty
QI (Qualifying Individual)	Part B premium only; must reapply yearly, granted first-come, first-served	Part B penalty
QDWI (Qualified Disabled & Working Individual)	Part A premium only, for certain working people with disabilities who lost premium-free Part A	Part A penalty

A late-enrollment penalty is part of the premium it attaches to, so a program that pays a premium absorbs that premium's penalty along with it, for as long as the parent qualifies. The Part D penalty is not shown here because it is erased by Extra Help, not by an MSP.

Table 18.2 - Medicare Savings Programs, 2026 Federal Monthly Income and Resource Limits

Program	Individual income	Couple income	Individual resources	Couple resources
QMB	$1,350	$1,824	$9,950	$14,910
SLMB	$1,616	$2,184	$9,950	$14,910
QI	$1,816	$2,455	$9,950	$14,910
QDWI	$5,405	$7,299	$4,000	$6,000

Figures are the 2026 federal limits and are slightly higher in Alaska and Hawaii. Many states use higher limits or disregard certain income and resources, so a family should confirm with its own state. Re-verify these amounts each year, as they change annually.

Here is the point that matters most for the families in this book, and it closes a loop opened back in Chapter 14. When an MSP pays a parent's Part B premium, it pays the whole premium, and the late-enrollment penalty is part of that premium. So the MSP absorbs the penalty along with it. The same is true for a Part A premium and its penalty under QMB. A permanent Part B penalty that a family could not appeal away, the kind Chapter 14 described as lasting for life, simply stops being the family's problem for as long as the parent qualifies for the program. This is why Chapter 14 called the safety net the most powerful of the three ways to deal with a penalty. It does not argue the penalty away. It pays it.

Extra Help, and How It Erases the Part D Penalty

Extra Help, known formally as the Part D Low-Income Subsidy, does for drug costs what the MSPs do for premiums. It lowers or eliminates the Part D premium, reduces the deductible, and caps what a parent pays at the pharmacy counter to a few dollars per prescription. In 2026, it is available to people with income up to 150 percent of the federal poverty level, roughly $23,475 a year for an individual and about $31,725 for a couple, within resource limits that a family should confirm against the Social Security Administration's own figures, because the published numbers vary slightly by source.

And Extra Help carries the same power over the Part D penalty that the MSPs carry over the Part B penalty. A parent who qualifies for Extra Help has the Part D late-enrollment penalty erased for as long as they qualify. The permanent penalty from Chapter 14 becomes, in practice, no penalty at all.

One connection makes all of this easier, and it works in a specific direction worth understanding. There is no separate national MSP form filed with Social Security. Instead, when a parent applies for Extra Help through the Social Security Administration, the law requires SSA to forward that application to the state Medicaid office to begin the Medicare Savings Program determination, unless the parent declines. So a single Extra Help application can open the MSP door as well. The reverse connection holds too: a parent who qualifies for an MSP, or for full Medicaid, is automatically enrolled in Extra Help. Either way, the three penalties this book worked so hard to prevent can all be lifted: Medicaid or an MSP absorbs the Part A and Part B penalties inside the premiums they pay, and Extra Help erases the Part D penalty. None of the three is beyond relief.

When a Parent Cannot Get Premium-Free Part A

The programs above solve a problem this book has returned to again and again: the parent who reaches Medicare age without premium-free Part A. This parent has no forty-credit record of their own, no spouse's record to borrow from, and no realistic path to forty credits now. For them, Part A carries a monthly premium, $311 or $565 in 2026 depending on their credits. The premium is real, and the instinct is to avoid it by not enrolling. That instinct is the costly mistake, and the programs in this chapter are what defeat it.

The plan runs on two tracks. Track one is enrollment. Enroll in Part B and Part D on time, no matter what the parent decides about Part A, because those two penalties are permanent and they run separately from Part A. Chapter 14 explains why skipping enrollment to dodge the Part A premium starts penalties on Part B and Part D that the parent can never shed. Track two is the programs in this chapter. Handle Part A through QMB or full Medicaid, so the premium is paid for the parent and the penalty is absorbed, rather than paid out of pocket or triggered by delay. A parent who qualifies for QMB or full Medicaid never carries the Part A premium at all.

How the State Pays, and Why No One Is Left Out

Every state pays the Medicare premiums for a senior who qualifies for QMB or full Medicaid. This is true in all fifty states. States use one of two methods, and the method changes the timing, not whether the parent gets help. The two kinds of states have names.

Buy-in states: the parent can sign up for both Part A and Part B at any time of year, and the late-enrollment penalties are erased. Every state and the District of Columbia is a buy-in state except the group payer states listed below.

Group payer states: the parent signs up during the January-to-March window, known as the General Enrollment Period, or GEP, and the state pays the premium, including any penalty amount. The group payer states are Alabama, Arizona, Colorado, Illinois, Kansas, Kentucky, Missouri, Nebraska, New Jersey, New Mexico, South Carolina, Utah, and Virginia.

Either way, the Part A and Part B premiums get paid for a parent who qualifies. These state agreements change over time, so confirm your own state's current status with a benefits counselor or the state Medicaid office.

The sign-up uses a safe step called conditional enrollment. Because a parent must have Part A before the state can approve the help, but cannot afford Part A first, they sign up for Part A on the condition that the state approves QMB or full Medicaid. If the state approves, Part A begins, and the state pays. If the state does not approve, Part A never starts and no Part A bill is ever owed. In a buy-in state, the same buy-in also lets the state enroll the parent in Part B at any time, so neither part is locked to the January-to-March window.

Two things to know before you file:

This cannot be done through the standard online Medicare application. It has no conditional option. The parent must contact Social Security directly, by phone appointment or at a local office, and say plainly that they want to apply for conditional Part A enrollment in order to apply for the state QMB program. Ask for written confirmation of the filing and take it to the state Medicaid office.

Part B is not conditional. It begins right away and must be paid until the state's help starts, so the parent should be ready to cover Part B premiums for a short stretch.

A shortcut: in a buy-in state, a parent who already has Part B does not need the conditional step at all. They can apply for QMB directly at the state Medicaid office, at any time of year. This is one more reason to enroll in Part B on time.

Timing connects the two tracks. Enroll in Part B on time to protect it. Then, if the parent qualifies, use QMB or full Medicaid to pick up the premiums and clear the penalties. A parent who already followed the on-time Part B advice often has the simplest path of all, because in a buy-in state they can apply for QMB directly and skip the conditional step entirely. One caution holds it together: all of this depends on actually qualifying, and for a sponsored parent, deeming can block these need-based programs until the deeming exit, so the help may not be available right away. Deeming is covered in Chapter 7.

Medicaid and the Cost of Long-Term Care

Medicaid is the largest program in this chapter and the one that answers the question Chapter 17 left open: who pays for long-term care. Medicare does not pay for custodial long-term care. Medicaid does. For a parent who needs years in a nursing home or a memory-care unit, Medicaid is often the only thing between the family and an unlimited bill.

Because Medicaid is meant for people with very limited assets, a parent generally qualifies only after their countable assets have been spent down to a low limit, commonly around $2,000 for a single applicant, though the exact figure is set by the state. Income rules apply as well and also vary by state. This is the spend-down Chapter 17 described, the savings of a lifetime consumed by care until Medicaid takes over.

The federal government does protect the spouse who still lives at home, so that one partner's care does not leave the other destitute. Under the spousal impoverishment rules, the at-home spouse, called the community spouse, is allowed to keep a share of the couple's assets. In 2026, that protected amount, the Community Spouse Resource Allowance, falls within a federal band from about $32,532 at the minimum to about $162,660 at the maximum, with each state setting its own figure inside that band. A portion of the couple's income is protected for the community spouse as well. These protections are a genuine shield, and a family facing a nursing-home admission for one spouse should understand them before spending down anything.

Medicaid Long-Term Care Is Not Automatic

Meeting the income and asset limits does not by itself entitle a parent to Medicaid long-term care. Federal law requires a second, separate test. Alongside the financial gate, a parent must pass a functional gate, a level-of-care assessment showing they actually need the level of care a nursing facility provides. This is usually measured by how much help the parent needs with the activities of daily living, bathing, dressing, eating, moving, and using the bathroom. A parent who is financially eligible but does not yet need that level of care will not receive long-term-care coverage until they do. The requirement to conduct this assessment is federal, but the federal government does not impose a single nationwide test, so the exact assessment and the precise threshold vary by state. A family should confirm both gates, financial and functional, with its own state Medicaid office.

Legitimate Medicaid Planning, and the Line You Cannot Cross

Because the spend-down can consume an estate, families often ask whether savings can be arranged ahead of time so that not everything is lost. The answer is yes, but only within the law, and the distinction is one every family must understand clearly.

Legitimate Medicaid planning means lawful strategies, arranged well in advance and guided by an elder-law attorney, to position a parent's finances so the family is not left entirely unprotected. It is legal, it is common, and for many families it preserves something of what a parent hoped to leave behind. But it works only when done early, and the reason is a federal rule called the look-back period. When a parent applies for long-term-care Medicaid, the state reviews the previous sixty months, five full years, of financial records. Gifts or below-market transfers made inside that window trigger a penalty period during which the parent is ineligible for Medicaid, and the length of that penalty depends on how much was transferred, calculated by a figure the state sets. Transfers made more than five years before applying fall outside the window entirely. This is why the planning must happen years ahead to do any good.

This look-back applies only to long-term-care Medicaid. It does not apply to the Medicare Savings Programs, to Extra Help, or to regular Medicaid coverage. A family applying for QMB or Extra Help does not face a look-back at all.

The federal period is sixty months, but some states use a shorter window for certain kinds of long-term-care Medicaid, and these rules change.

New York, for example, has had no active look-back for its home-care Medicaid, though a shorter look-back has been enacted and is expected to phase in. California has moved its look-back rules more than once in recent years and currently applies a period shorter than the federal sixty months. The specific number in any one state can change, so don't lean on it. What matters is confirming the current look-back for your own state and the specific kind of care before relying on any figure.

The line a family cannot cross is the difference between planning and concealment. Hiding assets, backdating transfers, giving money away in secret shortly before applying, or lying on the application is fraud. It can trigger penalties, disqualification, and worse. There is a lawful path, and there is a line, and the safe way to walk the first without crossing the second is with a qualified elder-law attorney rather than a shortcut heard from a neighbor. See Chapter 19 for how to find the right professional.

How to Apply, and Where to Get Help

The three core programs in this chapter are applied for in different places, and the paths connect. A Medicare Savings Program is applied for through the state's Medicaid office, and Medicaid itself is applied for there as well, because both are state-run. Extra Help is applied for through the Social Security Administration, online or at a local office. Because an Extra Help application is forwarded to the state to start the MSP process, a family that applies for Extra Help has often begun the MSP application at the same time without filing anything extra. A family unsure where to start can turn to the State Health Insurance Assistance Program, a free counseling service in every state that helps seniors understand and apply for exactly these programs.

The single most important message about these core programs is that the doors exist and that a family must knock to open them. None of them arrives on its own. A parent who qualifies for QMB will keep paying the Part B premium and its penalty until someone applies. A parent eligible for Extra Help will keep overpaying at the pharmacy until the application goes in. The programs are generous, but they are not automatic, and the family that learns they exist has already done the hardest part.

Beyond these three cost-help programs, two more programs can help on the income side by putting money in a parent's pocket rather than paying a Medicare cost. They are Supplemental Security Income and the totalization agreement, and the rest of this chapter covers each.

Supplemental Security Income

Supplemental Security Income, or SSI, can add to monthly income and open the door to Medicaid at the same time. It is a monthly cash benefit for people who are aged, sixty-five or older, blind, or disabled, and who have very low income and few assets. In 2026, the federal benefit is $994 a month for an individual and $1,491 for a couple, and some states add a supplement on top. The asset limits are low: $2,000 for an individual and $3,000 for a couple. SSI is applied for through the Social Security Administration, online, by phone, or at a local office.

SSI matters in this chapter for a reason beyond the cash. In most states, a parent who qualifies for SSI is automatically enrolled in Medicaid, and the SSI application doubles as a Medicaid application. So for a parent who qualifies, SSI can be the single door that opens both a monthly check and full Medicaid coverage, including the premium help and the long-term-care coverage described earlier in this chapter.

For immigrant parents, though, SSI carries a hard limit that families must understand before they count on it. SSI has strict noncitizen rules, and for many humanitarian immigrants, the benefit is time-limited. Refugees, people granted asylum, and certain other humanitarian categories can generally receive SSI for only seven years after their entry or grant of status. When those seven years run out, the SSI payments can stop, even for an elderly or disabled parent who still needs them, unless the parent has by then become a citizen or met another qualifying condition. This seven-year cliff has cut off vulnerable parents who did not see it coming. A family in this situation should treat naturalization as urgent, because citizenship removes the time limit, and should get advice well before the seven years end.

SSI is also the program most exposed to sponsor deeming. For a sponsored parent, the sponsor's income can be counted against SSI and block it until the deeming exit, which is covered in Chapter 7. A parent turned down for SSI because of deemed income should ask about the indigence exception before accepting the denial.

SSI is also one of the few benefits that counts for public charge. Unlike Medicare, Medicaid, the Medicare Savings Programs, and Extra Help, which do not count, SSI is treated as cash assistance and can weigh against a parent who later applies for a green card or seeks to return from a long trip abroad. A family should understand this exposure before applying. How public charge works, what it can and cannot do, and who it never touches are all covered in Chapter 7.

One More Safety Net: Totalization for the Social Security Check

The last program in this chapter works like SSI on the income side, not by cutting a Medicare cost but by raising a parent's income. It is called a totalization agreement, and for an immigrant parent who worked part of a career abroad, it can turn years of foreign work into a real monthly Social Security check.

Here is the problem it solves. Social Security normally requires 40 credits, about ten years of U.S.-covered work, before it will pay a retirement benefit. Many immigrant parents arrive later in life and never reach ten years of U.S. work, even though they worked for decades in their home country. Without help, all of that foreign work counts for nothing toward a U.S. benefit, and the parent is left with no Social Security check at all.

A totalization agreement fixes this. Where the United States has such an agreement with a parent's home country, Social Security will combine, or "totalize," the parent's U.S. credits with the credits earned in that country to see whether the combined record is enough to qualify. If it is, the parent receives a partial U.S. benefit, prorated to reflect the share of the career actually worked under U.S. Social Security. A parent who could never qualify on U.S. work alone can, through totalization, qualify for a real monthly payment.

There is one threshold to meet. To have foreign credits counted this way, a parent must have earned at least six U.S. credits, roughly a year and a half of U.S. work, on their own record. Below that, there is nothing for the agreement to build on.

The agreement must also be with the parent's home country. As of 2026, the United States has totalization agreements in force with thirty countries, listed in the table below. A parent whose home country is not on this list cannot use totalization, and because the list grows as new agreements take effect, a family should confirm the current status with the Social Security Administration.

Table 18.3 - Countries With a U.S. Totalization Agreement in Force (2026)

Countries
Australia, Austria, Belgium, Brazil, Canada, Chile, Czech Republic, Denmark, Finland, France
Germany, Greece, Hungary, Iceland, Ireland, Italy, Japan, South Korea, Luxembourg, Netherlands
Norway, Poland, Portugal, Slovak Republic, Slovenia, Spain, Sweden, Switzerland, United Kingdom, Uruguay

One point must be stated plainly, because it is easy to misunderstand and the mistake is costly. Totalization helps only the Social Security cash benefit. It does nothing for Medicare. The credits combined under a totalization agreement do not make Part A premium-free. Premium-free Part A still requires 40 credits of actual U.S.-covered work, and foreign credits brought in through totalization do not count toward it. So a parent might qualify, through totalization, for a monthly Social Security check while still owing a premium for Part A. The two systems ask different questions, and totalization answers only the Social Security one. A family should never assume that qualifying for a Social Security benefit through totalization has also solved the Part A cost. It has not.

Action Checklist

- ☐ Know the programs and what each pays: Medicare Savings Programs pay the Part A and Part B premiums, Extra Help pays down Part D drug costs, Medicaid pays for what nothing else does, including long-term care, and SSI adds monthly income and can open the door to Medicaid.
- ☐ Treat every income and resource limit in this chapter as a reliable federal figure and still check the parent's own state, because many states use higher limits or disregard certain income and assets.

- ☐ Remember that an MSP paying the Part B premium absorbs the Part B penalty with it, and QMB does the same for a Part A premium and penalty. The penalty stops being the family's problem while the parent qualifies.
- ☐ Remember that Extra Help erases the Part D penalty while the parent qualifies, and that qualifying for QMB, SLMB, QI, or full Medicaid brings Extra Help automatically.
- ☐ For a parent without premium-free Part A, enroll in Part B and Part D on time regardless of the Part A decision, then use QMB or full Medicaid to pay the Part A premium and absorb the penalties. Use conditional enrollment for Part A when the parent does not yet have it, filing with Social Security in person or by phone, not the online application, then applying for QMB at the state Medicaid office. See Chapter 14 for why the Part B and Part D penalties are permanent.
- ☐ Know whether the parent lives in a buy-in state, where both parts can be enrolled any time, and penalties are erased, or a group payer state, where sign-up runs through the January-to-March window. Confirm the state's current status, because these agreements change.
- ☐ For long-term care, understand that Medicaid pays only after both a financial spend-down and a functional level-of-care assessment, and that the community spouse is protected by the federal spousal impoverishment rules.
- ☐ Understand that the five-year look-back applies only to long-term-care Medicaid, not to the Medicare Savings Programs, Extra Help, or regular Medicaid, and that some states use a shorter look-back that can change. Confirm the current rule for your state.
- ☐ Understand legitimate Medicaid planning: lawful, early, attorney-guided arrangement of a parent's finances, and never concealment or improper transfers, which are fraud.

- ☐ Apply for the core cost-help programs in the right place: Medicare Savings Programs and Medicaid through the state Medicaid office, Extra Help through the Social Security Administration. Get free help from the State Health Insurance Assistance Program, and bring in an elder-law attorney for long-term-care planning. See Chapter 19.
- ☐ For SSI, apply through the Social Security Administration. Remember the seven-year limit that applies to many humanitarian immigrants, treat naturalization as urgent before that window closes, and know that SSI is exposed both to sponsor deeming and to public charge, unlike most health benefits. See Chapter 7.
- ☐ Consider totalization for the parent's Social Security check. If the parent worked in one of the thirty agreement countries and has at least six U.S. credits, foreign and U.S. credits can be combined to qualify for a partial Social Security benefit, but remember this does nothing for Medicare and does not make Part A premium-free.
- ☐ Knock on the door, because none of these programs is automatic. A parent keeps paying premiums, penalties, and full drug costs until someone applies.

PART SIX · WHERE TO TURN FOR HELP

CHAPTER 19

Build Your Medicare Team

Priya thought she had finished. She had charted her mother's two clocks, confirmed the profile, chosen a foundation, and even mapped the bridge. Then she sat at her kitchen table with the folder open and realized she was about to make every one of these decisions alone, for a parent whose future depended on getting them right.

"I keep reading that I should talk to an agent," she told her counselor. "And an attorney. And maybe a financial planner. But I don't know who does what, who I pay, or who I can trust. How do I even start putting these people together?"

"You start by realizing you don't need one expert," the counselor said. "You need a small team, and each member does one part of the job. The trick is knowing which person to call for which question, and how to tell a good one from a bad one. Let's build the team."

Every chapter in this book has pointed to a person who could help: an agent for the coverage choice, an attorney for the deeming and long-term-care questions, a counselor for the free guidance. This chapter puts those people in one place. It explains who belongs on a family's Medicare team, what each one does, how each one is paid, and how to find people worth trusting. No family should carry the whole burden alone, and no single professional can handle all of it well. The goal is a team, matched to the specific work this book has laid out.

Why One Expert Is Not Enough

The single most common mistake families make is assuming one person can answer everything. The insurance agent who is excellent at comparing Advantage plans usually cannot advise on Medicaid spend-down. The elder-law attorney who handles deeming and asset protection does not sell drug plans. The financial planner who manages an estate rarely knows the enrollment penalty rules cold. Each of these is a real specialty, and the immigrant family's situation touches all of them at once, because it mixes coverage, eligibility law, and long-term financial risk in a way an ordinary Medicare case does not.

That is why the right model is a team, not a guru. A family that understands who does what can direct each question to the right person, avoid paying for advice they can get free, and catch the moment when one professional is quietly out of their depth. The rest of this chapter introduces the four core members and how to work with each.

The Medicare Agent

The Medicare agent is the member a family works with most, and the one this book has referenced most often. A good agent does three things, the same three named in the coverage chapters. They match the coverage to the parent's health, budget, and doctors. They screen out plans that fit poorly or are sold aggressively. And they coordinate the pieces- foundation, drug coverage, and supplemental plans- so nothing overlaps and no gap or penalty is left open.

The most important fact about an agent is how they are paid, because it changes how a family should read their advice. A Medicare agent is rarely paid by the family. The agent is paid a commission by the insurance carrier when a parent enrolls in a plan, and that commission is built into the plan whether or not a family uses an agent. In practical terms, this means an agent's help usually costs the family nothing directly, which is a genuine benefit, but it also means the agent has a financial interest in which plan is chosen. A family does not need to be suspicious, but it should understand the incentive and ask the right questions.

Two distinctions matter when choosing an agent. The first is between a captive agent, who represents a single insurance company and can only sell that company's plans, and an independent agent or broker, who represents many carriers and can compare across them. For most families, an independent agent is the better starting point, because the whole value of the agent is an honest comparison, and a captive agent can only show one company's shelf. The second is whether the agent knows the immigrant family's specific issues, including the residence rule, the bridge years, and dual-eligible D-SNPs. Many competent agents have never handled these questions. A family should ask directly whether the agent has worked with immigrant parents and understands the eligibility side, not just the plan side.

Good questions to ask an agent include how many carriers they represent, whether they are independent or captive, how they are paid and by whom, whether they have worked with sponsored or recently arrived immigrant parents, and whether they will still be reachable after enrollment when a problem arises. An agent who answers these plainly is usually one worth keeping.

The State Health Insurance Assistance Program

Before a family spends a dollar, it should know about the State Health Insurance Assistance Program, known as SHIP. This is a federally funded program that provides free, unbiased Medicare counseling in every state. SHIP counselors do not sell anything and are not paid on commission, so their guidance carries no product incentive at all. For a family that wants a neutral second opinion, or that cannot yet afford paid help, SHIP is the most valuable free resource in the entire Medicare system.

SHIP counselors can explain enrollment windows, compare plan types in general terms, help a family understand a penalty letter, and point toward the safety-net programs covered in Chapter 18. What they generally do not do is make a specific plan recommendation the way an agent does, because their role is education and neutrality rather than enrollment. The smartest families use both: SHIP for a neutral understanding of the landscape, and an agent to execute the enrollment. A family unsure whether an agent's advice is sound can bring the same question to SHIP and compare the answers.

The Elder-Law Attorney

The elder-law attorney is the specialist for the hardest legal questions in this book, and the two that matter most are deeming and long-term-care planning. When a sponsor's income threatens to block a parent's need-based help, when a family must understand sponsor repayment exposure, or when a parent facing long-term care needs their finances arranged legitimately before Medicaid, this is the professional who does that work. An agent cannot, and a family should not attempt it alone, because the rules are technical and the mistakes are expensive.

Unlike an agent, an elder-law attorney is paid by the family, usually at an hourly rate or a flat fee for a defined piece of work. This is real money, and it is the reason a family should bring the attorney in for the questions that genuinely need legal expertise rather than for everything. The deeming analysis, the indigence exception, legitimate Medicaid planning, and estate protection are worth an attorney's fee. Routine plan selection is not. A family should look for an attorney who specifically practices elder law or is a member of a recognized elder-law professional group, not a general practitioner, because this is a distinct and technical field.

The Financial Planner

The financial planner is the fourth member, and the one whose role varies most by family. For a family with meaningful savings, a planner helps decide how to pay for long-term care, whether a hybrid long-term-care policy fits, and how to protect an estate across the years of a parent's later life. For a family with very little to protect, a planner may not be needed at all, and the money is better spent on an elder-law attorney and the safety-net route. The planner earns their place when there are assets to arrange and choices to weigh, which is exactly the terrain of the legacy layer.

How a financial planner is paid deserves the same scrutiny as an agent. Some planners are fee-only, charging the family directly and taking no product commissions, which removes the incentive to sell a particular policy. Others are paid through commissions on the products they recommend, such as annuities or insurance. A family should ask directly which model the planner uses, because a fee-only planner's advice on a long-term-care product carries no built-in incentive, while a commission-paid planner's does. Neither is disqualifying, but the family should know before it acts.

How the Team Works Together

The four members are not called in all at once, and most families never need all four heavily. They are called in as the work requires, and the sequence usually follows the arc of this book. Early on, a family uses SHIP for free orientation and an agent to understand coverage. If the parent faces deeming or is heading toward long-term care, the elder-law attorney enters for the legal work. If there are assets to protect, the financial planner joins for the legacy decisions. The agent stays involved throughout for the annual coverage review, because plans change every year and a plan that fit last year may not fit this one.

The family remains the center of the team. No professional makes the decisions; each supplies the expertise for their piece, and the family, usually the adult child holding the folder, keeps the whole picture. This is the role Priya was stepping into at her kitchen table, not doing everything herself, but knowing which expert to call for which question and how to judge the answer. A family that understands the team can assemble exactly the help it needs, pay only for what genuinely requires paying, and lean on free resources for the rest.

Action Checklist

- ☐ Build a team, not a single expert. Coverage, eligibility law, and long-term-care finance are separate specialties, and the immigrant family's situation touches all of them.
- ☐ Start with SHIP, the free State Health Insurance Assistance Program, for neutral, commission-free Medicare counseling in your state. Use it for orientation and second opinions.
- ☐ Use a Medicare agent to match, screen, and coordinate coverage. Prefer an independent agent who represents many carriers over a captive agent tied to one company.
- ☐ Understand the agent is paid by the carrier, not by you, so their help usually costs nothing directly but carries a plan-selection incentive. Ask how many carriers they represent and how they are paid.
- ☐ Ask any agent whether they have worked with sponsored or recently arrived immigrant parents and understand deeming, the residence rule, and dual-eligible D-SNPs, not just plan selection.

- ☐ Bring in an elder-law attorney for the technical legal work: deeming, the indigence exception, sponsor repayment exposure, and legitimate long-term-care and Medicaid planning. Expect to pay a fee, and reserve the attorney for questions that truly need legal expertise.
- ☐ Choose an attorney who specifically practices elder law, not a general practitioner, because this is a distinct and technical field.
- ☐ Involve a financial planner when there are assets to protect and long-term-care funding to weigh. Ask whether the planner is fee-only or commission-paid before acting on any product recommendation.
- ☐ Call each member in as the work requires rather than all at once, and keep the agent involved for the annual coverage review, because plans change every year.
- ☐ Keep the family at the center. No professional decides for you; each supplies one piece, and you hold the whole picture.

Part Seven · Execute

Chapter 20

The Parent Interview

Every plan in this book rests on facts, and the facts live with your parent. Before you choose a coverage combination, calculate a penalty, or start a five-year clock, you have to know what is true. The parent interview is the one sitting where you gather every input the plan needs. Do it once, do it carefully, and the rest of the work becomes arithmetic. Skip it, or guess at the answers, and every step downstream inherits the mistake.

This chapter gives you the questions to ask, the reasons each one matters, and a way to run the conversation so your parent feels supported rather than interrogated.

Setting Up the Conversation

Treat this as a dedicated session, not just a passing question at dinner. Set aside an hour when your parent is rested and unhurried. Explain why you are asking: you are building a plan to protect their health coverage and their savings, and the questions, some of which touch on money, immigration, and health, are the raw material for that plan. If your parent is more comfortable in their first language, interview in that language, or bring in a trusted family member to help. Some of these topics are sensitive. Move slowly, and let your parent know there are no wrong answers.

The Twelve Questions to Ask

Use these twelve questions as your interview script. Ask them in order; each one feeds a later part of the plan. The sections that follow explain what each answer drives and where in the book it gets used.

1. What is your parent's date of birth and current age?
2. What is your parent's current immigration status, the date of becoming a lawful permanent resident (LPR), and the date of entry to the U.S.?
3. Who sponsored your parent's green card, and is that sponsor still alive and bound by the I-864?
4. Is your parent married, widowed, or divorced, and what is the U.S. work history of any current or former spouse?
5. How many years did your parent work in the U.S. with reported earnings? How many years did they work with reported earnings in their country of origin (or any other country)?
6. What country (or countries) did your parent work in before coming to the U.S.?
7. Is your parent currently working, and are they willing and physically able to work in reported employment for the next 1-10 years?
8. What is your parent's current annual household income, and what does that income consist of (Social Security, pension from abroad, your support, rental income, etc.)?
9. What are your parent's total assets, including property in the U.S. and abroad, savings, and any property still owned in their country of origin?
10. What state does your parent live in, and is a move likely in the next 5 years?
11. What is your parent's current health status, and are there any diagnosed serious or chronic conditions?

12. Does your parent maintain significant ties to their country of origin - property, family, or plans to spend extended time (3+ months) there?

Two mapping notes before you begin. Question 1 anchors the age-and-date-of-birth timeline that every enrollment window is measured against. Question 2 deliberately pairs immigration status with two separate dates, because the date of entry and the date of becoming a lawful permanent resident are often not the same, and it is the LPR date, not the entry date, that starts the two five-year clocks in Chapter 6.

The Immigration and Residence Facts

Start with status and dates. You need the exact date your parent became a lawful permanent resident, because that single date drives the two five-year clocks: the residence requirement for Medicare eligibility (Chapter 6) and the five-year bar on full Medicaid. Capture the immigration category as well, and keep the date of entry distinct from the green-card date. Families routinely blur the two, and the difference can move an eligibility date by years.

The Sponsorship Facts

Ask who sponsored the green card and whether that sponsor signed an Affidavit of Support (Form I-864). The affidavit creates deeming, the rule that counts the sponsor's income against the parent for means-tested programs (Chapter 7). You need to know whether the sponsor is still living and still bound, because deeming ends under specific conditions. This is often the single fact that decides whether a parent can reach Medicaid or a Medicare Savings Program.

The Work-History Facts

Premium-free Part A comes from 40 U.S. work credits, earned by the parent or available through a spouse's U.S. work record (Chapter 9). Ask how many years your parent worked in the U.S. with reported earnings, and do the same for any current or former spouse. Only U.S. work under Social Security builds these credits.

The spouse's foreign work does not help here, because a spouse's credits deliver premium-free Part A only through their own U.S. work record. The parent's own home-country work is worth noting for a different reason: a totalization agreement, covered in Chapter 18, may help the parent qualify for a Social Security cash benefit, though it never counts toward Medicare. Keep that distinction clear, so no one expects foreign work to produce premium-free Part A.

Finally, ask whether your parent is currently working, and whether they are willing and physically able to work in reported employment for the next one to ten years. A parent who is a few credits short may still be able to close the gap.

The Health and Disability Facts

Ask about current health and any diagnosed serious or chronic conditions. Most conditions do not change Medicare timing, but two do: ALS and end-stage kidney disease open a faster door to Medicare regardless of age (Chapter 10). Note dementia or any condition pointing toward long-term care, which shapes the third-layer planning in Part 5. Handle this section gently; it is the most personal part of the interview.

The Financial and Location Facts

A parent's income and assets decide eligibility for the means-tested programs that erase premiums and penalties: Medicare Savings Programs, full Medicaid, and Extra Help (Chapter 18). Ask for current annual household income and what it consists of - U.S. Social Security, a pension from abroad, your support, rental income, and so on. Ask for total assets, including savings and any property owned in the U.S. or in the country of origin, because foreign assets can count. Then ask what state your parent lives in and whether a move is likely in the next five years. Medicaid and Medicare Savings Program rules vary by state, and long-term-care spend-down works differently place to place, so consider location as part of the plan, not just a footnote.

The Home-Country Ties

Ask whether your parent keeps significant ties to their country of origin: property, close family, or plans to spend extended time - three months or more - there each year. Extended absences can interrupt the physical-presence side of the residence clock (Chapter 6) and can bear on public-charge considerations tied to the affidavit (Chapter 7). A parent who spends half the year abroad is running a different plan than one who does not, and you need to know that before you build it.

Setting the Profile

With the answers in hand, you can place your parent into one of the working profiles used throughout the book (Chapter 8): the Worker, the Late Arrival, the Sponsored Parent, the Spouse-Credit Parent. The profile is a shortcut; a parent can carry features of more than one. What matters is that the interview gives you the facts to choose the profile honestly, and to know where a parent's plan will need extra attention.

From Interview to Plan

The interview is the intake; the rest of the book is the treatment. Once you have captured these facts, hand them forward. The dates, documents, and deadlines feed the Document Vault and Five-Year Tracker (Chapter 21), and the citizenship timeline feeds the Citizenship Action Plan (Chapter 22). Nothing in the interview is wasted; every answer has a home.

- ☐ Set up a dedicated, unhurried session in your parent's preferred language.
- ☐ Capture date of birth and current age (Q1).
- ☐ Record immigration status, the LPR date, and the date of entry, keeping the two dates distinct (Q2).
- ☐ Identify the sponsor and confirm whether the I-864 affidavit is still binding (Q3).
- ☐ Gather the parent's U.S. work years and any spouse's U.S. work history for premium-free Part A (Q4, Q5).
- ☐ Note the parent's own foreign work for the Social Security cash side only; it never counts toward Medicare (Q5, Q6).
- ☐ Ask whether the parent can and will work in reported employment for the next 1-10 years to close a credit gap (Q7).
- ☐ Record household income and its sources, and total U.S. and foreign assets, for means-tested program eligibility (Q8, Q9).
- ☐ Note state of residence and any likely move in the next five years (Q10).
- ☐ Ask about health and any serious or chronic conditions, flagging ALS and end-stage kidney disease and any long-term-care indicators (Q11).

- ☐ Ask about home-country ties and extended absences that could affect the residence clock and public-charge considerations (Q12).
- ☐ Set the working profile (Chapter 8) from the answers, then hand facts forward to the Document Vault (Chapter 21) and Citizenship Action Plan (Chapter 22).

CHAPTER 21

The Document Vault and Five-Year Tracker

The Document Vault and Five-Year Tracker

When the call came, David was ready. His mother had fallen, the hospital needed her Medicare and immigration details within the hour, and he did not have to search or guess. He opened one folder on his laptop, read off the permanent-residence date, the green-card number, and the insurance details, and it was done in minutes.

"A year earlier I'd have been tearing the house apart," he said. "Calling my sister, hunting for a shoebox of papers, hoping the green card was where I thought it was. Instead it was all in one place, and the one date the hospital needed was the same date the whole plan was built on. That folder is the reason I wasn't panicking."

The parent interview in Chapter 20 gathered the facts. This chapter gives them a home. A plan is only as good as a family's ability to find its pieces on the day they are needed, and that day rarely comes with warning. The document vault stores the papers. The five-year tracker watches the dates. Together they turn a one-time interview into a living system that protects the parent for years, not just on the afternoon the facts were first written down.

Why Storage Is Part of the Plan

Families treat gathering the facts as the finish line and storage as an afterthought. It is the opposite. The facts from the interview lose their value the moment they cannot be found, and the dates lose their value the moment a deadline passes unnoticed. A permanent-residence date written in a notebook that gets misplaced is no better than a date never gathered. The vault and the tracker exist so that the work of the interview keeps paying off long after the conversation ends.

There are two distinct jobs here, and they need two distinct tools. Documents are static; they need to be stored, protected, and findable. Dates are active; they need to be watched, because several of the most important events in this book- the two five-year marks, an enrollment window, a citizenship eligibility date- arrive on a schedule and punish a family that misses them. The vault handles the first job. The tracker handles the second. A family needs both.

Building the Document Vault

The document vault is a single, organized, secure place that holds every document the plan relies on. It can be physical, a labeled binder or file box, or digital, a set of folders backed up safely, or both, with the physical originals stored safely and digital scans kept as working copies. What matters is that it is one place, that more than one trusted family member knows where it is and how to reach it, and that it is secure, because these documents carry the sensitive identifiers that make identity theft possible. A vault left on an unsecured drive or in an unlocked drawer trades one risk for another.

The vault should be organized to mirror the interview, so that each fact gathered in Chapter 20 has a document behind it and a place to live. The following are the documents to collect and keep.

1. Immigration documents: the green card, front and back, the passport, any visas, and USCIS notices. These carry the permanent-residence date that starts both five-year clocks.
2. The Affidavit of Support, Form I-864, if the parent was sponsored, along with the sponsor's details, because this governs the deeming analysis.
3. The Social Security card and, once obtained, the Social Security earnings record, which is where the parent's actual work-credit count is confirmed.
4. Marriage, divorce, or death certificates for a spouse whose record may deliver premium-free Part A, because these prove the marriage details the credit rule depends on.
5. Proof of any foreign work history, for a possible totalization claim.
6. Medical and disability records, including any diagnosis relevant to the disability door, kept private but findable.
7. Financial records: income sources, asset statements, and property records in the U.S. and abroad, which the means-tested programs will require.
8. Once coverage begins, the Medicare card and all plan documents, so the current coverage is as findable as the eligibility papers.

A simple rule keeps the vault trustworthy: the document beats memory, always. When a fact and a paper disagree, the paper governs, and the vault is where the paper lives. A family that files each document as the interview surfaces it will finish the interview with the vault already half-built.

Building the Five-Year Tracker

The five-year tracker is the active half of the system, and it is named for the two five-year clocks that sit at the center of the immigrant family's whole situation. Its job is to convert dates into deadlines a family will actually notice in time to act. A date sitting in a document does nothing on its own. The same date, entered in a tracker with a reminder set well ahead of it, becomes a prompt to act while there is still time.

The tracker is built from the dates the interview produced, each one anchored to the permanent-residence date and the parent's age. The following are the events to track, each with a reminder set months ahead, not on the day itself, because most of these require action before the date arrives.

1. The five-year Medicare residence mark, five continuous years from the permanent-residence date, which opens the Medicare buy-in. See Chapter 6.
2. The five-year Medicaid bar lift, which opens full Medicaid, tracked from the same date but governed by its own rule. See Chapter 6.
3. The Medicare Initial Enrollment Period around the parent's sixty-fifth birthday, the seven-month window that avoids lifelong penalties. See Chapter 13.
4. Any Special Enrollment Period deadline, such as the eight-month window after employer coverage ends. See Chapter 13.
5. The citizenship eligibility date, generally five years as a permanent resident, which unlocks the most powerful moves in the book and feeds the plan in Chapter 22.
6. The deeming exit date, tied to citizenship or forty quarters, after which need-based help opens up. See Chapter 7.
7. The annual coverage review each fall, because plans change every year and a plan that fit last year may not fit this one. See Chapter 19.

The reminders are the point. A tracker that lists dates without alerts is just a second copy of the documents. Set each reminder far enough ahead that the family can act, several months before an enrollment window, a year or more before a citizenship eligibility date, so the deadline is met with room to spare rather than discovered as it closes.

How the Vault and Tracker Work Together

The two tools reinforce each other. The vault answers "where is the proof," and the tracker answers "when must we act," and almost every important moment needs both at once. When the residence mark arrives, the tracker signals the moment and the vault supplies the green card that proves the date. When the enrollment window opens, the tracker gives the deadline, and the vault holds the documents the application requires. When a hospital calls, as it did for David, the vault delivers the facts on the spot. Neither tool is sufficient alone. Together they make the plan operational.

This is also the system that catches a profile shift. When a new fact arrives- a confirmed credit count, a located marriage certificate, a citizenship eligibility date- it goes into the vault as a document and, if it carries a deadline, into the tracker as a dated event. The plan then adjusts, exactly as Chapters 8 and 12 described. The vault and tracker are how a plan stays current instead of freezing on the day it was made.

Keeping the System Alive

A vault and tracker built once and never revisited will slowly drift out of date. Set a standing time; the annual coverage review each fall is the natural moment to check that documents are current, that new papers have been filed, that reminders still point to the right dates, and that more than one trusted family member still knows how to reach the whole system. Update it whenever a document changes, a card is renewed, or a new fact is confirmed. The goal is a system that is trustworthy on the unplanned day, and that reliability comes only from small, regular upkeep.

The tracker also carries the single most important handoff in the book. The citizenship eligibility date it holds is the trigger for the citizenship action plan, because naturalization is the one move that collapses the residence rule, the welfare bar, deeming, and the SSI wait all at once. That plan is Chapter 22, and the tracker is what tells a family when to start it.

Action Checklist

- ☐ Storage is part of the plan, not an afterthought. Facts that cannot be found and dates that pass unnoticed are facts and dates wasted.
- ☐ Build one document vault, physical or digital or both, that is secure, backed up, and known to more than one trusted family member.
- ☐ Organize the vault to mirror the interview, so every fact from Chapter 20 has a document behind it: immigration papers, the Affidavit of Support, Social Security records, spouse certificates, foreign-work proof, medical and disability records, financial records, and, later, the Medicare and plan documents.
- ☐ Protect the sensitive identifiers in the vault, because these documents carry exactly what makes identity theft possible.
- ☐ Build a five-year tracker from the dates the interview produced, anchored to the permanent-residence date and the parent's age.
- ☐ Track the two five-year marks (Chapter 6), the Initial Enrollment Period and any Special Enrollment Period (Chapter 13), the citizenship eligibility date (Chapter 22), the deeming exit (Chapter 7), and the annual coverage review (Chapter 19).

- ☐ Set every reminder well ahead of its date, months before an enrollment window and a year or more before a citizenship eligibility date, so deadlines are met with room to spare.
- ☐ Use the two tools together: the tracker says when to act, the vault supplies the proof. Almost every key moment needs both.
- ☐ Feed every new fact back into the system, filing the document and, if it carries a deadline, adding the dated event, so the plan adjusts as facts confirm.
- ☐ Keep the system alive with regular upkeep, using the annual fall review to refresh documents, reminders, and access, and let the tracker's citizenship date trigger the plan in Chapter 22.

Part Seven · Execute

Chapter 22

The Citizenship Action Plan

Priya's mother almost didn't start. "I'm seventy-one," she said. "I've had my green card for twenty years. Why would I become a citizen now, at my age, with a test in a language that isn't mine?"

Priya had an answer, because the whole book had led to it. "Because it's the one thing that fixes everything at once, Ma. The waiting, the income rules that block help, all of it. And because of your age and how long you've been here, you may not have to take the test the way you're picturing. There's a version made for exactly you."

This is the last chapter, and it is the one that ties the whole book together. Again and again, across eligibility, deeming, the bridge years, and the safety net, one move kept appearing as the answer that dissolves the hardest problems. That move is citizenship. Every other strategy in this book manages a barrier. Citizenship removes the barriers. This chapter turns that recurring truth into a concrete, timed plan, so that a family does not merely know citizenship is powerful but actually gets their parent there.

One caution belongs at the very top of this chapter, because it applies to everything in it. The figures and rules below, the fees, the exemption ages, the residence periods, the process steps, are current as this book is written in 2026, but immigration fees and rules change often, and some are under active revision even now. Treat every number and rule in this chapter as a starting point, not a final answer. Before filing anything or making any decision that depends on a fee, an exemption, or a deadline, confirm the current rule at the official source, uscis.gov, or with an elder-law attorney or accredited immigration counselor. A rule that was true when this book was printed may have changed by the time you act on it.

Why Citizenship Is the Master Move

Throughout this book, the immigrant parent's difficulties trace back to a handful of barriers: the Medicare residence rule, the five-year Medicaid bar, sponsor deeming, and the long wait for SSI. Each chapter offered ways to manage or bridge these. Citizenship is different, because it does not manage them. It ends them. When a parent naturalizes, the residence rule no longer applies, the five-year Medicaid bar lifts, deeming ends, and the SSI wait is satisfied, all at once and permanently.

This is why citizenship has appeared in nearly every chapter as the single most powerful move. For the Late Arrival and the Sponsored Parent especially, it is the one event that can collapse an entire multi-year bridge into solid ground. A family that understands this stops seeing citizenship as a distant formality and starts seeing it as the central goal of the whole plan, the thing every bridge is buying time to reach. The bridge years exist to carry a parent safely to this door.

The Barrier That Feels Larger Than It Is

The reason many immigrant seniors never pursue citizenship is the fear Priya's mother voiced: the English and civics tests, taken late in life, in a language that is not the parent's own. That fear is real, and it stops families who would benefit most. But the fear is often larger than the actual rule, because the naturalization process contains exemptions built specifically for older, long-resident immigrants, exactly the parents this book is about.

Chapter 5 laid out these exemptions, and they are the heart of why an older parent should not rule out citizenship. As the rules stand in 2026, there are three that matter most for the parents in this book. Under the 50/20 exception, a parent who is age fifty or older at the time of filing and has been a permanent resident for twenty years is exempt from the English requirement and may take the civics test in their native language, with an interpreter. Under the 55/15 exception, a parent who is age fifty-five or older and has been a permanent resident for fifteen years gets the same relief: English-exempt, civics test allowed in the native language. And under the 65/20 special consideration, a parent who is age sixty-five or older and has been a permanent resident for twenty years is not only allowed to test in their native language but studies a reduced, designated set of civics questions rather than the full list.

The point is simply that the test a seventy-one-year-old with a twenty-year green card actually faces is very often not the test she is imagining. In her case, the 65/20 special consideration would let her study a short, marked set of questions and answer them in her own language. A family should confirm which exemption the parent qualifies for, and verify that these ages and residence periods still stand at the time of filing, before letting the fear of testing end the conversation.

The Timeline, and Why It Must Start Early

Citizenship is powerful, but it is not fast, and this is the fact that must shape the plan. Naturalization generally requires five years as a lawful permanent resident before a parent can even apply, along with a continuous-residence and physical-presence record across that period, and the application process itself takes many months from filing to the oath. A family that decides it wants citizenship on the day it needs the benefits has waited far too long, because the door does not open on demand. It opens on a timeline that must be started years ahead.

This is why the citizenship eligibility date belongs in the five-year tracker from Chapter 21, and why that date is the trigger for this plan. The permanent-residence date that starts the two five-year clocks also starts the clock toward naturalization eligibility. A family that tracked that date from the beginning already knows when the parent can apply. The plan, then, is to work backward from the eligibility date: prepare the parent, gather the documents, and be ready to file as soon as the door opens, rather than discovering the timeline only when a benefit is already out of reach.

Building the Action Plan

The citizenship action plan has a small number of concrete steps, taken in order, each one drawing on the system the last two chapters built. The interview supplied the facts, the vault holds the documents, and the tracker names the date. This plan puts them to work.

First, confirm the parent's eligibility date, five years from the permanent-residence date recorded in the vault, and read it off the tracker. Second, determine which testing exemption the parent qualifies for under the rules in Chapter 5, because that decides how the parent will prepare and removes the fear that stops most families. Third, gather the naturalization documents into the vault, since many are the same immigration papers already collected in the interview. Fourth, prepare the parent for the test they will actually take, whether the standard civics test, the civics test in their own language, or the reduced 65/20 set, using materials matched to their exemption. Fifth, file the application, Form N-400, as the eligibility date arrives, and track the steps that follow: the biometrics appointment, the interview, and the oath, each as a dated event in the tracker.

Cost should not silently end the plan either. As the rules stand in 2026, the naturalization filing fee for Form N-400 is $760 for a paper application or $710 to file online, and low-income applicants have two forms of relief. If your parent's household income is at or below 150 percent of the Federal Poverty Guidelines, they may qualify for a full fee waiver (Form I-912) and pay nothing. If their household income is above 150 percent but no more than 400 percent of the Federal Poverty Guidelines, they may instead qualify for the reduced fee of $380 (Form I-942). These fee amounts and relief options are exactly the kind of rule that changes, and a significant increase along with proposed limits on the reduced fee and waiver has been under consideration, so confirm the current fee and the current relief options before you file rather than relying on the figures printed here. A family that would benefit from citizenship but is worried about the cost should ask about any available reduction or waiver rather than abandon the plan, and an elder-law attorney or an accredited immigration counselor can advise on both the cost and the application itself.

When Citizenship Is Not the Right Move

Honesty requires naming the exceptions, because citizenship is not automatically right for every parent. Some parents have a genuine reason to retain only their green card, such as a home country that does not permit dual citizenship and assets or standing there they cannot give up. Chapter 5 weighed this cost and benefit in full, and a family that faces such a situation should return to that analysis. For a small number of parents, the honest answer is to remain a permanent resident and rely on the bridge and safety-net strategies the rest of the book provides.

These exceptions only count if they're genuine. Otherwise they're just the testing fear this chapter already addressed. For the large majority of immigrant parents, and especially for the Late Arrival and the Sponsored Parent carrying the heaviest barriers, citizenship is the move that does the most good. The right approach is to make the decision deliberately, with the real exemptions and the real trade-offs in view, rather than to let citizenship slip away by default.

The Last Word

This book began with an adult child overwhelmed by a system that seemed designed to defeat their immigrant parent. It ends here, with the one move that turns that system from an adversary into solid ground. Everything between, the two clocks, the profiles, the bridge, the layers, the safety net, is the work of protecting a parent through the years it takes to reach this door. Citizenship is where the plan is meant to arrive.

Priya's mother took the oath at seventy-two. The residence rule, the deeming, the years of careful bridging, all of it resolved on that single morning. She had feared a test in a language not her own, and in the end she answered a handful of civics questions in her own language and became a citizen. What her daughter remembered more than the paperwork was the fact that the worry was finally over, replaced by something permanent. That is what the citizenship action plan is for, and it is where a family's work, done well, is meant to end.

Action Checklist

- ☐ Treat every figure and rule in this chapter as current to 2026 but subject to change. Confirm fees, exemptions, and deadlines at uscis.gov or with an accredited professional before filing or deciding anything.
- ☐ Treat citizenship as the master move, the one event that ends the residence rule, the five-year Medicaid bar, deeming, and the SSI wait all at once, rather than managing each barrier separately.
- ☐ Do not let the fear of the English and civics tests end the conversation. Confirm which testing exemption the parent qualifies for under Chapter 5: the 50/20, the 55/15, or the 65/20 special consideration, because an older, long-resident parent often faces a far simpler test, taken in their own language.
- ☐ Read the parent's citizenship eligibility date off the five-year tracker from Chapter 21, generally five years from the permanent-residence date, and treat that date as the trigger for this plan.
- ☐ Work backward from the eligibility date, preparing the parent and the documents in advance, so the application is ready to file the moment the door opens rather than years after it was needed.
- ☐ Gather the naturalization documents into the vault, drawing on the immigration papers already collected in the interview.
- ☐ Prepare the parent for the specific test they will actually take, standard, in their own language, or the reduced 65/20 set, using materials matched to their exemption.
- ☐ File Form N-400 as the eligibility date arrives, then track the biometrics appointment, the interview, and the oath as dated events.

- ☐ Ask about the reduced fee or the full fee waiver if cost is a barrier: the full waiver for income at or below 150 percent of the Federal Poverty Guidelines, and the reduced fee for income above 150 percent but no more than 400 percent. Confirm the current fee and current relief options first, because these have been proposed for change. Consider an elder-law attorney or accredited immigration counselor for the fee and the application. See Chapter 19.
- ☐ Make citizenship a deliberate decision. If a parent has a genuine reason to keep only the green card, return to the cost-benefit analysis in Chapter 5, but do not let that be a cover for the testing fear.
- ☐ Remember the bridge years exist to carry the parent to this door. Citizenship is where the plan is meant to arrive.

Medicare 101 Reference

This reference gathers, in one place, the definitions and figures the rest of the book relies on. It is meant to be used, not read straight through: when a term or a number comes up in a chapter, this is where to confirm what it means. Every figure here is current to 2026 and, like all Medicare figures, changes annually. The premiums, deductibles, and income limits below are reset each year, so confirm any number against the official source, medicare.gov or ssa.gov, before acting on it. Where a topic has a full treatment elsewhere in the book, this reference points to the chapter that carries it.

The Four Parts of Medicare

Medicare is built from four parts, each covering a different kind of care, and much of the book turns on how they fit together.

1. Part A, hospital insurance, covers inpatient hospital stays, skilled nursing care after a hospital stay, some home health care, and hospice. It is premium-free for a person with enough work credits and carries a premium for those without. Building toward premium-free Part A is the subject of Chapter 9.
2. Part B, medical insurance, covers doctor visits, outpatient care, preventive services, and durable medical equipment. It

carries a monthly premium for nearly everyone and pays about eighty percent of covered costs, leaving the rest to the beneficiary.

3. Part C, Medicare Advantage, is a private plan that delivers Part A and Part B benefits together, usually with Part D drug coverage and extra benefits bundled in, and adds an out-of-pocket cap. It is one of the three coverage roads in Chapter 15.
4. Part D, prescription drug coverage, covers medications, either as a standalone plan added to Original Medicare or built into a Medicare Advantage plan.

Two more terms complete the picture. Original Medicare means Part A and Part B together, the government program a person can pair with a standalone Part D plan and, optionally, a Medigap policy. Medigap, also called a Medicare Supplement, is private insurance that pays costs Original Medicare leaves behind, most importantly the Part B twenty percent. Medigap cannot be combined with a Medicare Advantage plan; a family chooses one road or the other, as Chapter 15 explains.

Key 2026 Figures

The following are the figures the book refers to most often, gathered for quick reference. All are 2026 amounts and all change annually.

Table A.1 Premiums and core cost figures, 2026

Item	2026 amount
Part A premium, 40+ credits	$0 (premium-free)
Part A premium, 30–39 credits	$311 per month
Part A premium, fewer than 30 credits	$565 per month
Part B standard monthly premium	$202.90
Part D national base beneficiary premium	$38.99
Medicare Advantage in-network out-of-pocket maximum, legal cap	$9,250
Medicare Advantage average in-network out-of-pocket maximum	about $5,421

Note on figures still to confirm at print: the Part A inpatient hospital deductible and the Part B annual deductible are standard 2026 amounts that this book does not use in any calculation, so they are omitted here rather than printed from an unverified value; if you want them in the reference, they should be confirmed against medicare.gov first. The Part A premium tiers above are tied to work-credit counts, where forty credits earn premium-free Part A, thirty to thirty-nine credits carry the lower premium, and fewer than thirty carry the higher one, as detailed in Chapter 9.

The Enrollment Periods

Medicare has several enrollment windows, and missing the right one is what triggers the penalties in Chapter 14. The main ones are these.

1. Initial Enrollment Period (IEP): the seven-month window around the sixty-fifth birthday, the three months before the

birthday month, the birthday month, and the three months after. This is the primary window, covered in Chapter 13.

2. General Enrollment Period (GEP): January 1 through March 31 each year, for those who missed their IEP. Enrollment through the GEP can carry a late penalty. It is also the enrollment window used by group-payer states in the buy-in process described in Chapter 18.
3. Special Enrollment Period (SEP): a window opened by a qualifying event, most importantly the eight-month period after employer coverage from current work ends, which lets a person enroll in Part B without penalty. See Chapter 13.
4. Annual coverage review, each fall, the open enrollment window for changing Medicare Advantage and Part D plans, and the natural time for the yearly plan check described in Chapter 19.

The Safety-Net Programs

For families who cannot afford the premiums, several means-tested programs pay costs and, in some cases, erase penalties. These are the subject of Chapter 18; the definitions below are the quick reference.

1. Medicare Savings Programs (MSPs): state programs that pay Medicare premiums for low-income beneficiaries. QMB is the broadest, paying both Part A and Part B premiums plus cost-sharing; SLMB and QI pay the Part B premium; QDWI helps certain working disabled people with the Part A premium.
2. Full Medicaid: for those who qualify, pays premiums and cost-sharing much as QMB does, covers long-term custodial care, and serves as the entry point to a Dual Eligible Special Needs Plan.

3. Extra Help, also called the Part D Low-Income Subsidy (LIS): reduces or eliminates Part D premiums and copays and erases the Part D late-enrollment penalty.
4. Supplemental Security Income (SSI): a monthly cash benefit for low-income aged, blind, or disabled people that, in most states, opens the door to Medicaid automatically.

Terms That Recur Through the Book

A handful of terms appear across many chapters and are worth defining in one place.

1. Work credit (or quarter): the unit that counts toward premium-free Part A and Social Security. Forty credits, roughly ten years of work, earn premium-free Part A. See Chapter 9.
2. The two five-year clocks: the five continuous years of permanent residence that open the Medicare buy-in, and the five-year bar before full Medicaid. Both run from the permanent-residence date. See Chapter 6.
3. Deeming: the rule that counts a sponsor's income as available to a sponsored parent, which can block need-based help until it ends. See Chapter 7.
4. Affidavit of Support (Form I-864): the sponsor's binding pledge of financial responsibility, the document that triggers deeming. See Chapter 7.
5. Public charge: the immigration test that can weigh certain benefits, notably cash assistance such as SSI, against a person in some immigration decisions, while most health programs do not count. See Chapter 7.
6. Creditable coverage: drug coverage at least as good as Part D. Keeping creditable coverage avoids the Part D penalty; a gap

of 63 or more continuous days without it triggers the penalty. See Chapter 14.

7. IRMAA (income-related monthly adjustment amount): a surcharge added to the Part B and Part D premiums for higher-income beneficiaries, calculated on the standard base. It is referenced in the penalty math in Chapter 14.
8. Conditional Part A enrollment: applying for premium Part A so that it takes effect only if the state approves premium payment through QMB or Medicaid, so no bill is owed if help is denied. See Chapter 18.
9. Buy-in and group-payer states: the two ways states handle premium payment for QMB or Medicaid beneficiaries; buy-in states allow enrollment any time, while group-payer states use the General Enrollment Period. See Chapter 18.
10. Totalization agreement: a treaty that lets work credits from another country combine with U.S. credits toward a Social Security benefit, though not toward premium-free Part A. See Chapter 18.

The Three Layers of Dignity, at a Glance

The book's coverage framework, Part 5, builds in three layers, each answered by its own chapter.

1. Dignity I, Foundation: the choice of how to build on Part A and Part B, through Original Medicare with Part D, Medicare Advantage, or Original Medicare with Part D and Medigap. See Chapter 15.
2. Dignity II, Protection: the supplemental plans that pay cash, hospital indemnity, critical illness, cancer, and dementia coverage, filling the gaps the foundation leaves. See Chapter 16.

3. Dignity III, Legacy: planning for long-term care, the largest cost of all, through savings, private insurance, or Medicaid. See Chapter 17.

A Final Word on Every Number Here

Medicare is re-priced every year. The premiums, deductibles, income limits, and thresholds in this reference are 2026 figures, and they will shift for 2027 and beyond. The rules can change too, sometimes substantially. Use this reference to understand what a term means and roughly what a figure is, then confirm the current number at medicare.gov or ssa.gov, or with a knowledgeable agent or benefits counselor, before making any decision that depends on it. The definitions age slowly. The numbers age every January.

Where to Check Before You Act

The rules in this book were accurate as of 2026, but Medicare, Social Security, and immigration rules change often. Before you make any decision for your parent, confirm the current rule at one of the official sources below. When something is unclear, talk to a qualified professional - the kind this book points you to.

Medicare Medicare.gov - enrollment, coverage, plan comparison, and current costs. 1-800-MEDICARE (1-800-633-4227) - general Medicare questions, 24 hours a day.

Social Security & Work Credits SSA.gov - retirement, disability, survivor benefits, and your parent's earnings record. Social Security also handles Medicare enrollment for most people.

Immigration & Citizenship USCIS.gov - green card, naturalization, sponsor and public-charge rules.

Free, Local Medicare Help Your State Health Insurance Assistance Program (SHIP) offers free, unbiased Medicare counseling. Find your state's office at shiphelp.org, or ask at your local senior center or Area Agency on Aging.

Medicaid & State Programs Medicaid.gov - an overview of Medicaid and the Medicare Savings Programs. Because Medicaid is run state by state, search for your own state's Medicaid agency for the rules that apply to your parent.

One habit worth keeping: whenever you read a number or a rule anywhere - including in this book - check the date attached to it. In this field, a fact without a date is only half a fact.

About the Author

Lawrence Lee is a Medicare professional and registered Insurance Continuing Education (CE) Provider in multiple states, with twenty years of corporate insurance strategy and training experience in Korea and the United States. He began his career in Medicare as a teacher of agents - and soon became the person those agents called when they hit a case no one else could solve.

Those hardest cases almost always came from the same place: immigrant families trying to navigate a system that was never built with them in mind. That pattern shaped his life's work. Lawrence came to see that there are really two Medicare worlds - the familiar one for lifelong U.S. seniors, and a second, far more punishing territory of residence clocks, sponsor rules, waiting periods, and public-charge fears, where knowledgeable help is scarce and honest resources are almost nonexistent. This book is his attempt to close that gap.

As a registered CE Provider and instructor, he trains agents at every stage - from newcomers to seasoned veterans - to understand not just what to do, but why each part of the Medicare system exists and how to navigate it ethically and with genuine cultural awareness. Through a weekly webinar series covering Medicare, Medicaid, and Social Security, he keeps hundreds of agents current in a rapidly changing field. His guiding belief is simple: when advisors truly understand the whole system - especially its complexity for immigrant seniors - they stop selling plans and start becoming advocates for the communities that need them most.

Lawrence is the founder of New American Family Advisors. You can reach him through New American Family Advisors.

Acknowledgments

To my parents and my family, who have always believed in me - thank you. Everything I am able to do begins with you.

My thanks to my daughter Hannah, who proofread the manuscript and gave it its final polish.

To Jongjoon Kim, founder of Smart Insurance, and Tony Holland, founder of Global Premier Benefits - thank you for inspiring me to write this book. Your encouragement turned an idea I had carried for years into something real.

To all the agents I have worked with over the years: thank you. I came to teach you, but I learned just as much in return. Your questions and your toughest cases showed me where the real gaps were.

To the immigrant seniors and families who let me into their situations - thank you. While I was helping you, you were teaching me. It was in those moments that I saw clearly the gap this book is meant to fill.

And to you, the reader - thank you for trusting this book with something as important as your parents' care. I hope it serves you well.

Lawrence Lee

Contact New American Family Advisors

Thank you for reading. If this book helped you, I would love to hear about it, and to help where I can.

New American Family Advisors exists to help immigrant families navigate Medicare, and to train the advisors who serve them. If you have a question about your parent's situation, or you'd like to know more about the resources mentioned in this book, you can reach me here:

Email: info@newamericanfamilyadvisors.net
LinkedIn: https://www.linkedin.com/in/lawrence-lee-995844b/

For agents, agencies, carriers, FMOs, and community organizations: if you're committed to helping immigrant seniors get the Medicare guidance they deserve, I'd welcome the conversation. I offer accredited continuing-education training and a webinar series on Medicare and the three layers of dignity for seniors. Reach out through the contact information above.

If this book was useful to you, a short review on Amazon helps another family find it. Thank you for that, and for the trust you placed in these pages.

Lawrence Lee

NAFA
New American Family Advisors